Evaluating Navy's Funded Graduate Education Program

A Return-on-Investment Framework

Kristy N. Kamarck, Harry J. Thie,
Marisa Adelson, Heather Krull

Prepared for the United States Navy
Approved for public release; distribution unlimited

 NATIONAL DEFENSE RESEARCH INSTITUTE

The research described in this report was prepared for the U.S. Navy. The research was conducted in the RAND National Defense Research Institute, a federally funded research and development center sponsored by the Office of the Secretary of Defense, the Joint Staff, the Unified Combatant Commands, the Department of the Navy, the Marine Corps, the defense agencies, and the defense Intelligence Community under Contract W74V8H-06-C-0002.

Library of Congress Cataloging-in-Publication Data

Evaluating Navy's Funded Graduate Education Program : a return-on-investment framework / Kristy N. Kamarck ... [et al.].
    p. cm.
  Includes bibliographical references.
  ISBN 978-0-8330-5033-5 (pbk. : alk. paper)
  1. United States. Navy—Officers—Education (Graduate)—Evaluation. 2. United States. Navy—Officers—Education (Graduate)—Costs. I. Kamarck, Kristy N.

  V411.E82 2010
  359.0071'173—dc22

                                                          2010029613

The RAND Corporation is a nonprofit institution that helps improve policy and decisionmaking through research and analysis. RAND's publications do not necessarily reflect the opinions of its research clients and sponsors.

RAND® is a registered trademark.

Published 2010 by the RAND Corporation
1776 Main Street, P.O. Box 2138, Santa Monica, CA 90407-2138
1200 South Hayes Street, Arlington, VA 22202-5050
4570 Fifth Avenue, Suite 600, Pittsburgh, PA 15213-2665
RAND URL: http://www.rand.org/
To order RAND documents or to obtain additional information, contact
Distribution Services: Telephone: (310) 451-7002;
Fax: (310) 451-6915; Email: order@rand.org

Preface

The military services send substantial numbers of their officers to graduate school. The cost of a graduate school billet, coupled with the cost of the schooling itself, imposes a considerable financial burden on the services. Therefore, they are interested to know whether the return on their investment warrants the cost of the education. The RAND National Defense Research Institute (NDRI) was asked to conduct an assessment of the quantitative and qualitative returns on investment (ROIs) for funded graduate education for naval officers. This monograph reviews the evolution of Department of Defense (DoD) and U.S. Navy policy with respect to funded graduate education and the metrics used to evaluate Navy graduate education programs and those within the other services. The document provides an ROI framework for evaluating the benefits and costs of providing funded graduate education. The authors presume some knowledge of the terminology associated with officer management, education evaluation, and ROI. The monograph should interest the military manpower, personnel, training, and education community. Comments are welcome and may be sent to Harry_Thie@rand.org.

This research was sponsored by the Navy and conducted within the Forces and Resources Policy Center of the RAND National Defense Research Institute, a federally funded research and development center sponsored by the Office of the Secretary of Defense, the Joint Staff, the Unified Combatant Commands, the Navy, the Marine Corps, the defense agencies, and the defense Intelligence Community.

For more information on RAND's Forces and Resources Policy Center, contact the Director, James Hosek. He can be reached by email at James_Hosek@rand.org; by phone at 310-393-0411, extension 7183; or by mail at the RAND Corporation, 1776 Main Street, P.O. Box 2138, Santa Monica, California 90407-2138. More information about RAND is available at www.rand.org.

Contents

Figures

Tables

Summary

Background, Purpose, and Approach

The U.S. Navy and the other military services send a number of their officers to graduate-level institutions each year to obtain advanced degrees. The primary purpose of providing these officers graduate education is so they can fill positions in their services whose duties require the knowledge and skills gained in graduate school. Furthermore, the benefits of a graduate education extend beyond the specific assignment for which the officer was educated, applying to subsequent assignments as well, albeit less directly. However, at an estimated cost of about $245,000 per officer for a funded master's degree, the cost of this education is substantial. For fully funded education, the service must pay not only the cost of the education but also the pay and allowances associated with an officer's billet allocated for education. Additionally, an opportunity cost is incurred: While the officer is attending school, his or her services are lost to the operational billets in which he or she could be gaining experience. The question frequently arises as to whether the benefit gained from a graduate education is worth the cost. While the quantitative effects of graduate education can be estimated, evaluating the qualitative effects of a graduate education poses a number of challenges.

The Navy asked NDRI to assess the quantitative and qualitative ROI for funded graduate education. The NDRI research team reviewed the educational policies of DoD and the Navy, compared the Navy's programs and metrics with those of the other services, and did a detailed analysis of two officer communities within the Navy: surface warfare and meteorology and oceanography.

Findings

Key findings from the research include the following:

- **DoD educational policy suggests broader and more extensive use of graduate education than simply filling billets that have been determined to require it.** The new DoD policy speaks to educating military personnel for "future capabilities." While the Navy's most recent policy guidance on graduate education *governance* appears to accord with the DoD policy, it is not clear that this broader view has permeated the Navy's educational community. The Navy's system for managing graduate education and the metrics it uses to evaluate the performance of that system tend to focus on filling validated billets—that is, it manages to meet present needs, not to build future capabilities.
- **Graduate education provides both technical skills and non-technical competencies or "soft skills," which are valued in a wide range of Navy billets beyond those that require graduate education.** The Navy realizes additional value through improved officer productivity, better decisionmaking, and increased retention. Additionally, in certain billets, competencies gained in graduate education may compensate for lack of domain knowledge.
- **Cross-service differences exist in graduate education philosophy; program parameters; utilization rates; and, particularly, program management.** The Navy has one of the largest requirements for graduate education in terms of annual quotas and validated billets. It has 550 annual quotas to fill some 4,800 billets, compared with the Air Force's 460 quotas and the Marine Corps' 180 quotas for far fewer billets each.[1] It also has the lowest uti-

---

[1]   In Navy terminology, *quota* refers to an individual billet for a training or education course. Navy program managers control a discrete number of quotas for each program, which they

lization rates for officers with graduate education among all the services. The Navy's average career utilization rate for non–staff corps officers is about 50 percent, compared with the Air Force's nearly 60 percent within one tour following graduation and the Marine Corps' 96 percent. Moreover, even if the Navy achieved better utilization rates, there is still a mismatch between validated billets and graduate school quotas in the Navy.

- **Differences exist among Navy communities in the management of officers and billets that require graduate education, particularly between the restricted line and unrestricted line communities.** The restricted line has proportionally more billet requirements, more-frequent utilization, and more-frequent reutilization than the unrestricted line community. Cultural influences and career demands within the unrestricted line often impede demand for graduate school and service in validated billets.

- **Education execution, billet execution, and officer management execution are decentralized, and incentives and penalties for billet and quota management are not integrated.** Community managers and education program managers often have different goals and metrics for assessing program success. Community managers focus on operational issues and gauge their success by how well they fill all the billets in the fleet. Education managers focus on filling graduate school quotas with qualified officers and on placing officers with the proper educational credentials in validated billets. At times these goals clash, with the result being unfilled billets or billets filled by individuals who do not have the requisite experience or qualifications.

- **The overall benefits in terms of ROI to the Navy from graduate education can be measured, given certain assumptions.** Although assessing the qualitative effects of graduate education poses some challenges, it is possible to make some reasonable assumptions about the costs and benefits of a graduate education. Our approach presents a way to ascertain the costs and

---

can allocate to individuals. Typically, the individual's command will request a quota for a specific program, and the program manager will either approve or disapprove the request.

some assumptions to determine benefits. These parameters can be adjusted in the model to identify elements that are particularly sensitive. An order-of-magnitude estimate is quite feasible, and more precise assessment would be possible with better data.

- **The current metric, which specifies one utilization per career for each educated officer as specified in the DoD and Navy instructions, will not give the Navy a break-even ROI within a 20-year career, given our assumptions.**
- **Recouping the investment in graduate education expenses based on skills gained requires long service by officers in billets requiring the graduate education (multiple utilization tours) and even longer service in other billets.**

Recommendations

In light of our findings, we have divided our recommendations into three areas: policy, culture, and monitoring and evaluation.

Policy

To bring Navy educational practices more in line with DoD policy to shift graduate education toward development of future capabilities, the Navy needs to introduce a top-down approach to replace the bottom-up one it now employs. This shift would include reviewing existing graduate education instructions to verify that the language and intent square with current DoD policy. Navy policymakers should consider the intent of DoD policy (DoD Instruction 1322.10), revised in April 2008, that "Knowledge is good, and more is preferable." Once this policy language is clear, Navy leaders need to communicate their graduate education policy to graduate education program managers, community managers, and officers.

Justifying the cost of graduate education requires extremely long service. However, the value of graduate education might be perceived to lie in the increasing productivity and decision quality that its soft skills and general knowledge provide. If so, the education may be considered a cost of doing business to achieve future capabilities. Moreover, if developing future capabilities is the program goal, it seems justifiable to make graduate education a competitive selection for those most likely to stay in the service and advance to flag rank. In essence, the Navy would be broadly educating many to achieve future capabilities and an ROI from the few.

Culture

Increasing emphasis on graduate education as a benefit to the community and to the Navy at large will require a cultural shift for some Navy communities to overcome negative perceptions about career "breaks" for education and utilization assignments. In line with a top-down approach, community leaders should set goals for graduate education attainment. One example might be "90 percent of all officers advancing at the O-5 board will have a graduate degree." In tandem, community leaders need to develop goals for the types of graduate degree curricula that would support their anticipated capability requirements beyond their current validated billet requirements.

The Navy can take some tactical steps to improve their utilization efficiency immediately by increasing utilization rates and reutilizing officers with advanced degrees, thus increasing net quantitative ROIs. The Navy should provide incentives for more-integrated management of officer assignments at the community level and also institute penalties for poor management of billets, quotas, and officers.[2] These should vary by community to reflect differences in billet structures and operational requirements. Community leaders should also seek to provide incentives for completing graduate educations and serving in validated billets to increase economic returns on their education investments. The Navy should consider the approach the Air Force uses, which includes master's degrees in promotion decisions. Additionally, because officers who serve in subsequent assignments that require graduate degrees increase the Navy's net benefit in terms of ROI, promotion boards and

---

[2] One option for penalizing poor management would be a loss of graduate education quotas for communities that fail to meet certain threshold utilization rates for officers in validated billets.

other incentive initiatives should give exceptional weight to those who have both an advanced degree and practical experience in a given field.

Monitoring and Evaluation

The Navy should expand its utilization metric and enhance monitoring and evaluation of its graduate education program. The one-tour utilization metric needs to take into account additional benefits to the Navy that officers with graduate education offer. In particular, using these officers in billets not coded as requiring a graduate degree may offer value that graduate education program managers are not currently capturing. Better data collection and periodic evaluations of graduate education programs under a hierarchy of outcomes would assist in identifying this value.

Conclusion

The Navy possesses the necessary mix of institutions and curricula in its funded graduate education program to meet its present capability requirements. However, the metric of one utilization tour, as defined in current Navy policy, is not capturing the total value of graduate education to the Navy. In fact, given the current graduate school timing and career progression for most officers, one utilization tour per educated officer does not recoup the cost of educating that officer within a 20-year career. Our research and analysis indicate that the knowledge and skills gained through graduate education are valuable for both the officer and for the Navy. The value for the Navy lies in improved productivity, better decisionmaking, and increased retention. Some of this value can be monetized, and costs and benefits to the Navy can be estimated using enhanced data-collection methods and reasonable assumptions. Recent shifts in DoD policy language and intent suggest that the Navy should expand on the one-tour utilization metric to establish a more-nuanced assessment of the value of graduate education for the Navy's officer corps, especially with respect to future capabilities.

Acknowledgments

This research benefited from the input of manpower and education experts from each of the services, who talked with us and shared valuable data and insights. We take responsibility for the analysis herein but also appreciate the collaboration and support of LCDR Claude McRoberts, CAPT Karen Emmel, CDR Darin Evenson, CAPT John Coronado, CDR Rob Tortora, CAPT Richard Moyer, LCDR Joseph Scott, LCDR Bart Fabacher, and LCDR Bradley Andros, USN; Maj. Bradley Ward, USMC; Scott Lutterloh, Vicki Poindexter, Marilyn Augustine, Steve Muir, and Richard Linton, OPNAV N15; William Hatch, NPS; Roelene Freeman, USA HRC; and Maj Ann Igl and Capt Michael Sukach, USAF. We are also grateful for the support of CDR Richard Haberlin, CAPT Eric Kaniut, LCDR Scott Snyder, CAPT Karen Schriver, Arthur Barber, and Linda Lester from our sponsoring office.

This project also benefited from the assistance of RAND colleagues Margaret Harrell, Sheila Kirby, and Kevin Brancato.

We are indebted to our reviewers, Lawrence Hanser of RAND and Jennie Wenger of the Center for Naval Analyses, for their thoughtful comments and improvements. We also appreciate the help of RAND's Beth Asch for her guidance and Jerry Sollinger for his contributions to the summary and editing.

Abbreviations and Glossary

AAD	advanced academic degree
ADSO	active-duty service obligation
AFIT	Air Force Institute of Technology
AMOS	additional military occupational specialty
BUPERS	Bureau of Naval Personnel
CIVINS	civilian institution
DoD	Department of Defense
DoDI	Department of Defense instruction
IGE	immediate graduate education
MA	master of arts
MAcc	master of accounting
MBA	master of business administration
MCO	Marine Corps order
METOC	meteorology and oceanography
MOS	military occupational specialty
MS	master of science
NDRI	National Defense Research Institute

NPS	Naval Postgraduate School
NWC	Naval War College
O-1	ensign (Navy), second lieutenant (Air Force, Army, Marine Corps)
O-2	lieutenant, junior grade (Navy), first lieutenant (Air Force, Army, Marine Corps)
O-3	lieutenant (Navy), captain (Air Force, Army, Marine Corps)
O-4	lieutenant commander (Navy), major (Air Force, Army, Marine Corps)
O-5	commander (Navy), lieutenant colonel (Air Force, Army, Marine Corps)
O-6	captain (Navy), colonel (Air Force, Army, Marine Corps)
OPNAV	Office of the Chief of Naval Operations
OPNAVINST	Office of the Chief of Naval Operations instruction
P code	code designating an officer having a funded master's degree and a billet requiring such an officer
pol-mil	political-military
Q code	code designating an officer holding a funded master's degree plus experience in the relevant subspecialty and a billet requiring such an officer
quota	in Navy terminology, an individual billet for a training or education course
R code	code designating an officer holding a doctorate
RL	restricted line
ROI	return on investment

ROTC	Reserve Officer Training Corps
SEP	special education program
STA-21	Seaman to Admiral-21 Program
SWO	surface warfare officer
URL	unrestricted line
USNA	United States Naval Academy
VGEP	Voluntary Graduate Education Program
YOS	years of service

CHAPTER ONE

Introduction

The U.S. Navy and the other military services provide training and education as part of their officer development programs. For the Navy, this model includes opportunities to gain knowledge and skills in a graduate school and apply them to various assignments at sea and ashore. The Navy funds graduate education with the expectation that the officers chosen to receive it will go on to apply the knowledge and skills they acquire in billets (positions) for which that education is a prerequisite. The officers selected for this education are typically in grade O-3 (lieutenant) and will use their education starting in grade O-4 (lieutenant commander) and continuing throughout their careers.

Purpose

The RAND National Defense Research Institute was asked to assess qualitative and quantitative measures for return on investment (ROI) for funded officer graduate education. While Navy graduate education is a combination of fully funded, partially funded, and unfunded programs, our focus was on funded programs at the Naval Postgraduate School (NPS), at the Air Force Institute of Technology (AFIT), and at civilian graduate institutions. Our review did not include graduate programs provided at institutions that are part of professional military education, such as the Naval War College (NWC).

Department of Defense and Navy Educational Policy

This section reviews past and present Department of Defense (DoD) and Navy policies for funded graduate education. In general, current policies take a broader view of educational requirements for officers.

DoD Policy

DoD Instruction (DoDI) 1322.10, revised in April 2008, requires that graduate education be established to accomplish the following goals:

- Raise professional and technical competency and develop future capabilities.
- Provide developmental incentives for military officers with the ability, dedication, and capacity for professional growth.
- Fulfill a present need, anticipated requirement, or future capability.

The previous version of DoDI 1322.10 took a narrower view, specifying that the purpose of funding graduate education was to fill billets that required that education. The new instruction represents a philosophical break from the previous directive, in that its view of the value of graduate education is much more expansive (see Table 1.1). In the words of a DoD official responsible for the policy, "knowledge is good, and more of it is preferable."[1] This change in philosophy resulted from the experiences of the military after September 11, 2001, when it encountered difficulty in finding officers having the broad range of backgrounds and academic disciplines needed for transformation, and for stability, transition, and reconstruction operations. Recent testimony from many individuals before Congress continues to call for a more-qualified and broadly educated officer corps.[2]

---

[1] RAND researcher interview with DoD official in July 2009. He did not say that he wished to be anonymous, but we typically start interviews by saying that comments will not be attributed.

[2] See, for example, Lt. Gen. (ret.) David W. Barno and Professor Williamson Murray, testimony to the House Armed Services Subcommittee on Investigation and Oversight, September 10, 2009.

Table 1.1
Changes to DoD Policy

Old DoDI 1322.10 Aug 26, 2004	New DoDI 1322.10 April 29, 2008
4.1 It is DoD policy to fund graduate education fully and partially for active-duty military officers required to fill Military Service requirements for validated positions.	4.1 The intent of the Department's graduate education programs are to provide fully or partially funded educational opportunities in disciplines that fulfill a present need, anticipated requirement, or future capability and that contribute to the effectiveness of the Military Departments and the Department of Defense.

The new DoD instruction did not remove the requirement to use officers who had attended graduate school at government expense in positions having specific educational requirements. However, the instruction does require the services to provide biennial reports to DoD that include three elements. The first assesses utilization and outcomes. This includes a review of validated billets, the number of officers who have obtained funded graduate education, an evaluation of their utilization rate in validated billets, and the number of utilization tours served. While the first element focuses on utilization in validated billets, the second and third elements are broader assessments of graduate education management. The second discusses management of officers who have had a graduate education. Beyond the utilization figures, how is the service managing (e.g., assigning, retaining, promoting) this pool of developed human capital? The third assesses the service posture with respect to disciplines that fulfill present needs, anticipated requirements, or future capabilities.

Navy Policy
The Navy also has a new instruction specifically pertaining to graduate education governance, which was issued after the new DoD instruction. The older instruction, Office of the Chief of Naval Operations (OPNAV) Instruction (OPNAVINST) 1520.23B (1991), provides general guidance on graduate education programs and states that the Navy offers graduate education to

- support requirements for officers with specific subspecialty skills[3]
- encourage professional knowledge and technical competence
- provide recruitment and retention incentives
- recognize aspirations of individuals.

The more-recent instruction, OPNAVINST 1520.42 (2009), which provides guidance for the integrated governance of graduate education programs, states that education is a strategic investment in the future capabilities of the naval service and that education policies should develop a portfolio of skills and competencies necessary to execute Chief of Naval Operations guidance and maritime strategy.[4]

Research Approach

Our approach to the research consisted of four tasks. The first was to review the civilian and military literature concerning graduate education and its returns. The second was to compare the funded graduate education programs across the services to identify additional metrics used to measure ROI. The third was to analyze data to understand demand (billets) and supply (educated officers) and how they matched, then to use these data as a basis for a model that allowed community-level assessments of utilization. The fourth was to posit and assess measures of ROI. The central question we are addressing is, "Is there value to the Navy in providing funded graduate education?" The use of the language of return of investment is meant to imply use of an ROI framework but not a complete ROI assessment.

---

[3]   Subspecialties will be discussed later in more detail. Beyond the staff corps, Navy communities have approximately 100 subspecialties falling into six broad areas. The subspecialties themselves resemble academic disciplines.

[4]   The extent to which the Navy has institutionalized this more-liberal policy is unclear.

Limitations

As stated earlier, we did not assess all graduate education programs in the Navy but only those funded for NPS, AFIT, and civilian institutions for unrestricted line (URL) and restricted line (RL) officers. Moreover, we did not attempt to ascertain which institutions should provide the education or the costs and benefits associated with using particular institutions or relying on their curricula to provide education. We did not provide a complete assessment of ROI at the program-budget level but instead offer a rough order-of-magnitude assessment for the sponsor or those responsible for education to use as a framework.

Organization of This Monograph

The monograph has six chapters. Following this introduction is a detailed review of the civilian and military literature. Chapter Three discusses the specifics of the Navy program and compares it with other military services. Chapter Four presents community-level data and our observations from running a utilization model. Chapter Five is our assessment of qualitative and quantitative benefits and costs in an ROI framework. Chapter Six contains our conclusions and policy recommendations. Additional material that may be of interest to some readers is in the appendixes.

CHAPTER TWO

Literature Review

This chapter discusses civilian and military literature on the theories and empirical evidence linking graduate education to organizational benefits. Figure 2.1 shows the possible benefits of graduate education by categories. The first section of this chapter discusses human and social capital development theory in relation to organizational returns. The second section takes a closer look at the contributions cited in civilian and military literature on quantifiable organizational returns. Finally, the chapter discusses various approaches for evaluating ROI and develops a hierarchal framework for measuring benefits from graduate education in the Navy.

Figure 2.1
Possible Benefits of Graduate Education to the Navy

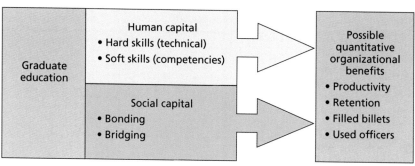

Theories Linking Graduate Education to Human and Social Capital

This section reviews the theoretical literature on human and social capital and how they can benefit organizations.

Human Capital Theory

To discuss ROIs with respect to education, researchers often start with education's effect on the development of human capital. Increases in human capital, in turn, may generate both pecuniary and nonpecuniary returns for an organization. *Human capital* is often defined as the set of acquired knowledge, skills, and capabilities that enable individuals to act in new ways (Coleman, 1998).

The skills gained from education can generally be divided into two types: hard skills and soft skills. *Hard skills* include technical capabilities that are directly applicable to specific tasks, for instance, data analysis, financial accounting, electrical engineering, or undersea warfare. John McPeck (1994) describes hard skills as being "knowledge based" because their "general range of applicability is limited by the form of thought being called upon" (McPeck, 1994). Studies have found that these of types of vocational skills tend to degrade over time without frequent use or the additional education needed, in part, because of exogenous technological changes.

Soft skills, on the other hand, are not explicitly taught during graduate education but instead are competencies gained through the process of being educated, sometimes called "learning to learn." These types of skills include critical thinking, communication, and leadership. While soft skills are less tangible, they help individuals "select pertinent information for the solution of a problem [and] formulate relevant and promising hypotheses" (McPeck, 1994). Table 2.1 compares hard and soft skills.

The civilian literature is unclear on how education develops soft skills, but these skills are strongly and positively correlated with schooling (see, for example, Oreopoulos and Salvanes, 2009; Boyatzis, Stubbs, and Taylor, 2002; and Hardison and Vilamovska, 2009). Some evidence also specifically suggests that graduate education increases

Table 2.1
Comparison of Soft Skills and Hard Skills

Human Capital: Hard Skills	Human Capital: Soft Skills
Skills	
Data analysis	Communication
Drafting	Critical thinking
Modeling	Team-building
System analysis	Creativity
Design	Decisionmaking
Financial accounting	
Skill attributes	
Knowledge based	Process based
Degrade over time without use	Increase with experience
Easier to define, measure, and test	Difficult to define, measure, and test
Technical degrees offer specific gains	All degree curricula offer gains

soft skills that are valuable to the Navy. The services have used competency models to define characteristics of high-performing officers. One example is the Navy Leadership Competency Model, which defines five core competencies: accomplishing the mission, leading people, leading change, working with people, and resource stewardship.[1] Additionally, competencies that are deemed critical for Navy flag officer billets are closely related to some of the skills developed through graduate education (see Table 2.2). A study of naval officers who had completed a graduate degree at NPS found significant increases in the officers' own assessments of gains in seven out of ten skill areas that are closely tied to competencies desirable for chief executive officers (Filizetti, 2003).

The evidence also indicates that skill gains from graduate education have benefits beyond utilization in subspecialty billets. Opinion surveys of naval officers having a graduate degree found that over 90 percent of the individuals who had served in billets requiring graduate degrees reported that the skills gained in their education were nec-

---

[1] The Navy Leadership Competency Model is available on the Air Force Air University's Strategic Leadership Studies website.

Table 2.2
Competencies Are Critical in Navy Billets

Critical Flag Officer Billet Requirements[a]	Competencies Gained at NPS[b]	Competencies Gained in MBA[c]
Influencing and negotiating with people at all levels	Communications	Persuasiveness Negotiating Networking Oral communication
Preparing and delivering quality oral presentations and written communication	Communications Computer and information Technology use	Oral communication Written communication
Exercising good judgment, perception, adaptability, and common sense to integrate priorities and eliminate irrelevant information	Ability to define and solve problems Analytical reasoning Technical adaptability Research and continuous learning	Flexibility Self-control Attention to detail Use of concepts Efficiency orientation
Motivating, inspiring, and mentoring military personnel	No significant gain in collaboration and teamwork	Group management Developing others' empathy
Guiding expectations, managing risk, and achieving results	Systems thinking and analysis Innovation and creativity	Planning Efficiency orientation Systems thinking

[a] Hanser et al., 2008.

[b] Filizetti, 2003.

[c] Boyatzis, Stubbs, and Taylor, 2002.

essary or desirable for performing their duties, while over 80 percent said that they used their education in billets other than the designated ones (Cashman, 1994).

Competencies gained through education, regardless of curriculum, may also help to compensate for lack of domain knowledge in certain billets. In a study of senior Air Force officers and civilians, Scott et al. (2007) found that leaders use such competencies as people skills, problem-solving, integration skills, and enterprise knowledge in billets for which they lacked a technical background or functional expertise.

Social Capital Theory

Social capital development is closely tied to human capital and is widely assumed to be a by-product of education. *Social capital* is most commonly defined as the "networks, norms and trust—that enable participants to act together more effectively to pursue shared objectives" (Putnam, 1995, p. 665). Social capital comprises both the individual's network and the assets that may be mobilized through that network (see, for example, Nahapiet and Ghoshal, 1998). Putnam (1995, p. 667) found that education is one of the biggest contributors to the development of social capital:

> Highly educated people are much more likely to be joiners and trusters, partly because they are better off economically, but mostly because of the skills, resources, and inclinations that were imparted on them at home and in school.

> There is no consensus on how to measure social capital, but it is believed to help improve productive and allocative efficiency by increasing information-sharing, promoting cooperative behavior, and reducing monitoring costs by increasing trust.

Social capital can be broken down further into "bonding" social capital and "bridging" social capital. *Bonding social capital* refers to networks that form inside an organization; *bridging social capital* refers to connections among heterogeneous groups (Schuller, Baron, and Field, 2000). Bonding social capital might have negative effects if it builds "in-group" solidarity at the expense of outsiders (Fukuyama, 2002). Additionally, tightly bound groups may cut themselves off from information, innovation, or ideas with negative consequences for the organization. Bridging social capital, on the other hand, tends to increase social inclusion and encourage connections and cooperation between people from different walks of life. These ties tend to be more fragile because they require active reinforcement to maintain, but some consider them to be more valuable than homogeneous bonds (Schuller, Baron, and Field, 2000).

In the Navy context, graduate education can affect both bonding and bridging social capital. For example, while obtaining a graduate degree at NPS, an officer is sacrificing time he or she could be spending in an operational billet in his or her community, which may reduce "in-group" bonding capital. However, the officer will likely develop ties to officers in other Navy communities, other branches of the U.S. military, even with officers in foreign militaries. These bridging connections may be more useful in future joint assignments or in combined coalition operations. Officers who obtain a degree at a civilian institution may be exposed to an even broader set of viewpoints and may develop connections with future civilian policymakers.

Organizational Benefits of Graduate Education

Economists use two general models to describe how increases in human and social capital generate organizational returns. First, the productive efficiency model suggests that, as skills increase, individuals are able to get more done in the same amount of time for the same amount of money. This result might be tied to improved multitasking or to time management skills. Second, the allocative efficiency model suggests that more-skilled individuals make better decisions than do less skilled people facing similar circumstances.

While human and social capital are not directly measurable, they do lead to quantifiable benefits for an organization. The civilian literature on organizational returns to graduate education quantifies human and social capital gains through changes in productivity. Increasing employee productivity in the private sector leads to increases in profitability for a firm. In the military, increasing individual or unit productivity can likewise lead to pecuniary benefits by reducing manpower requirements and improving readiness (Mehay and Bowman, 2007). Therefore, the military literature on returns from graduate education focuses on education's effect on officer performance, promotion, and retention.

The civilian literature crosses a broad range of sectors and degree types, although the bulk of the literature focuses on primary and secondary education. A large portion of the literature on ROI from graduate education in the military comes from research surveys and empirical studies that students and faculty at NPS, AFIT, and other service colleges have produced.

Civilian Literature

It is difficult to quantify individual productivity gains from education. Brown (2001, p. 1) states that

> One of the problems with measuring training's influence on worker productivity is that there are many areas of productivity that are intangible and difficult to quantify, such as ideas, abilities, experience, insight, motivation and so forth.

Another problem with measuring productivity gains has to do with selection bias. Individuals who attend and complete graduate education may have innate abilities that would make them more-productive workers even in absence of a graduate degree. This means that simply comparing individuals having graduate educations with those who do not without controlling for innate ability would overstate the benefits of that education. However, researchers have found that the positive effects of graduate education exist apart from selection effects.

Generally, the civilian literature quantifies individual productivity increases through salary differentials between graduate-degreed employees and comparable employees without graduate degrees. These salary differentials are a proxy for expected worker productivity gains and vary by the type of degree obtained and the sector of employment. Typically, the "funder" reaps the reward; in the private sector, the employee typically has made the initial investment for graduate education, and the ROI accrues to the individual through increased earning potential. The employer in turn pays a premium for the expected productivity gains from the education the individual has funded.

Various studies on earnings data have found individual rates of return between 7 and 46 percent, with returns generally higher for individuals who have earned a master of business administration (MBA) or technical master's degree. A 2008 study on ROI to an MBA for information technology professionals found that these individuals earned 46 percent more than those with only bachelor's degrees and 37 percent more than those with sector-specific master's degrees (Mithas and Krishnan, 2008). If the individual does a full-time MBA degree, forgoing two years of work experience, the ROIs are 36 percent relative to a bachelor's degree and 27 percent relative to a technical master's degree (Mithas and Krishnan, 2008).

Firms in the private sector also measure productivity by increases in profitability. Black and Lynch (1996) found that the average educational level of a firm's employees has a positive and significant effect on productivity in both the manufacturing and nonmanufacturing sectors and that this positive influence was higher in the nonmanufacturing firms (Black and Lynch, 1996).

Hunton, Stone, and Wier (2005) conducted one of the largest empirical studies of the effects of graduate education on professional success and tacit knowledge learning. The researchers combined standardized job performance evaluation data for approximately 6,000 accountants with survey data from around 3,000 members of the sample to compare the performance, problem-solving ability, and managerial knowledge of those with and without an MBA or master of accounting (MAcc) degree. Those with MBAs and MAcc degrees demonstrated significantly higher knowledge gains and performance evaluations than the employees who lacked advanced degrees. The authors also found that the MAcc degree is more beneficial for early and midcareer, and the MBA is more beneficial later in a career.[2]

Military Literature

The military's human resource structure is characterized by an internal labor market, a vertical hierarchy, and a closed personnel system (Asch and Warner, 1994). Military officer pay is determined by rank and time in service, regardless of the officer's educational qualifications; officers with graduate degrees do not earn more. Therefore, quantifying productivity increases in the military is more difficult than it is in the

---

[2] Although Hunton, Stone, and Wier focused on the private sector, generalizing their results to the military might suggest that focusing on technical degrees may be more useful for officers early in their careers (O-4 to O-5), while degrees with a broader focus, such as the MBA, might benefit officers in grades O-6 and above.

private sector. Various studies have used performance ratings as a proxy for individual productivity. Although performance ratings are thought to be highly inflated, researchers have identified useful performance metrics. In a Navy study on the effects of college quality on performance, Bowman and Mehay (2002) used the "recommendation for accelerated promotion" indicator on the officer's fitness report to identify highly productive performers. The authors found that the quality of the educational institution does not have a significant effect on performance ratings for staff officers. However, line officers with graduate degrees from either public or private top-tier colleges had significantly higher performance ratings in their early careers than their peers from less-selective institutions.

Increased promotion potential is typically considered an individual, rather than organizational, benefit. However, military studies have also used years to promotion and probability of promotion as proxies for increased productivity, which would benefit the organization. Faster promotion or higher promotion rates are assumed to equate to increased individual productivity. Branigan (2001) found that naval officers who have had funded graduate degrees have shorter times to promotion than have officers lacking graduate degrees. Bowman and Mehay (1999) found that officers with graduate degrees are more likely to be selected for promotion at the O-4 promotion boards than their counterparts without graduate degrees. However, a large portion of the relationship between graduate education attainment and promotion is due to unobserved attributes that may lead more-promotable officers to attend or be selected for graduate school (Bowman and Mehay, 1999).

For the organization, increasing retention provides quantifiable benefits: reducing recruitment and training costs and supervisory time (Fitz-Enz, 2000). Private corporations that pay for all or part of their employees to attend graduate school often stipulate a minimum contract term following graduation, which directly increases short-term retention rates. As with productivity, a selection bias might also affect the retention results, although it is not clear whether the net effect would be to overestimate or underestimate retention figures. An employee who accepts education funding might be predisposed to staying with the organization and may be "signaling" these intentions by entering a graduate program. This effect may be greater in the military, which imposes an additional service obligation on graduate students; thus, "a positive preference for graduate school should be positively correlated with retention" (Bowman and Mehay, 2002). Alternatively, individuals who are predisposed to leaving an organization may pursue graduate education to increase their marketability to external employers (Jordan, 1991).

Military studies generally show a positive retention effect from funded graduate education. Opinion surveys of naval officers having less than eight years of service (YOS) who had received funded graduate education indicate that 80 percent planned to stay in the Navy for 20 years or longer (Cashman, 1994). Jordan (1991) estimated that URL officers having a graduate degree were less likely to leave the military before their O-4 promotion boards than their counterparts lacking a graduate degree and that this retention effect was more pronounced for officers having NPS degrees than for officers having degrees from other sources. Milner (2003) found that United States Naval Academy (USNA) officers who received master's degrees through the Voluntary Graduate Education Program (VGEP) were more likely to remain in the service at the end of their initial commitments than were USNA officers lacking a master's degree. In a similar study, Mehay and Bowman (2007) found that officers who had benefitted from immediate graduate education (IGE) had retention rates 25 percent higher than those of their counterparts lacking education out to seven YOS and 10 percent higher out to ten.

Approaches to Evaluating Graduate Education Benefits

The theory and empirical evidence outlined in the previous sections demonstrate the positive organizational benefits to be gained from graduate education. Employers who sponsor education and training are, however, particularly interested in ways to quantify these benefits to make efficient programming decisions. The literature on the best way to determine the ROIs for education and training has been growing.

Understanding the concept of ROI analysis begins with understanding the evaluation methodologies behind it. One of the most common models was adapted from an existing model for evaluating training and development efforts. This adapted model includes five progressively complex levels of evaluation (U.S. Government Accountability Office, 2003):

1. reactions—focused on opinions of an education program; participant's response to the program
2. learning—focused on amount of knowledge gained from the program
3. application—focused on link between learning and changes in on-the-job behavior
4. impact—focused on the effect of the education program on the organization's performance
5. ROI—compares the benefits (as quantified in dollars) to the costs of the education program.

Table 2.3 suggests a hierarchy of measures for the Navy, including recommended data collection tools and assessment frequency.[3] Although the higher assessment levels may allow more-precise calculation of net benefits, they also require more-complex analysis, such as longitudinal studies, and thus may be more costly to conduct. Therefore, we recommend conducting these assessments only every three to five years. Moreover, many of these assessments could be accomplished as student theses. At the lower levels of assessment, it may be cost-effective to track performance continuously, and net positive feedback at these levels of assessment would imply that the education program is providing value to the organization.

Jack Phillips has suggested four steps that organizations should take when moving along this hierarchy of assessment measures toward an ROI calculation (Phillips, Stone, and Phillips, 2001). The first step is to collect data to prepare for the evaluation through surveys, observations, or other methods. Appendix B includes a further discussion

---

[3] Appendix B includes more specific recommendations for data tracking and analysis.

Table 2.3
Hierarchy of Suggested Measures

Levels of Assessment[a]	Data Collection Tools	After Degree	1st Tour After Degree	After Utilization Tour	Biennial Report	3–5 years
Reaction						
1. Satisfaction with program	a. Opinion surveys (Did you like the program?)	X	X	X		
Learning						
2. Knowledge or skills gain	a. Pre- and post-tests	X				
	b. Opinion surveys (Did you gain knowledge/ skills from the program?)	X	X	X		
Application						
3. Effective utilization	a. Number of subspecialty billets filled				X	
	b. Number of funded officers in subspecialty billets				X	
	c. Billets vs. inventory				X	
	d. Billet fit (exact vs. matrix match)				X	
	e. Opinion Surveys (Did you use knowledge/ skills in billet?)		X	X		
4. Efficiency of utilization	a. Time to first utilization tour				X	
	b. Utilization in a career				X	
	c. Reutilization				X	

Table 2.3—Continued

Levels of Assessment[a]	Data Collection Tools	After Degree	1st Tour After Degree	After Utilization Tour	Biennial Report	3–5 years
Impact: organization						
5. Retention	a. YOS beyond degree award					X
	b. YOS beyond ADSO					X
	c. YOS career (active and reserve)					X
6. Performance in billet	a. Supervisor surveys			X		
	b. Fitness reports (graduate education vs. non–graduate education)					X
7. Contribution to strategy and policy	a. Thesis topic				X	
	b. Thesis quality				X	
Impact: officer						
8. Promotion	a. YOS to promotion (O-4, O-5, and O-6)					X
9. Career satisfaction	a. Career satisfaction surveys	X	X	X		
10. Marketability	a. Salaries for Navy retirees					X
ROI: benefits versus costs						
11. Billet program cost	a. Number of billets x cost of billet				X	

Table 2.3—Continued

Levels of Assessment[a]	Data Collection Tools	After Degree	1st Tour After Degree	After Utilization Tour	Biennial Report	3–5 years
12. Education program cost	a. Number of funded quotas x cost of funded quota				X	
13. Economic return	a. Community review using utilization data				X	

[a] Our levels of assessment are adapted from a four-level model for evaluating training programs and the Government Accountability Office's five-level model (2003). We sought measures that met the criteria of being complete and usable and of conveying understanding.

of recommended practices for data collection and analysis. The Navy already collects personnel data and can both improve and expand the educational variables that it tracks.

The second step is to isolate educational effects. This step can be achieved through subjective assessments by managers and former students on how education might change measurable outcomes. The literature suggests a number of methods for testing competency gains through both self-assessments and external assessments. The examples listed below are from Boyatzis, Stubbs, and Taylor, 2002, and Hardison and Vilamovska, 2009:

- **self-assessments**
  - Learning Skills Profile—individuals rate 72 skill statements on levels from 1 (no skill) to 7 (leader and creator)
  - Self-Assessment Questionnaire—72 questions assessing 21 competencies
- **external assessments**
  - External Assessment Questionnaire—given to boss, colleagues, peers, etc., to assess competencies
  - Critical Incident Review—an observed interview evaluating 16 different competencies
  - Group Discussion Exercise—an observed simulation; participants are given a set of 3 problems and must talk through their recommendations to their chief executive officer (16 competencies evaluated)
  - Presentation Exercise—an observed presentation with a question-and-answer session
  - Critical Learning Assessment—rated tasks requiring students to apply several aspects of critical thinking, including problem solving, analytic reasoning, and written communication skills.

The third step is to monetize the data on education effects by assigning values to the education outcomes predicted in step two and calculating an annual program value. The direct educational costs and the opportunity costs should also be monetized in this step. Finally,

ROI is calculated by dividing the estimated value of the education by its cost.

In the next two chapters, we take a closer look at the Navy program parameters and data, and in Chapter Five, we use existing community-level data to build an ROI framework for the Navy's education program.

CHAPTER THREE

Navy Program and Service Comparisons

Graduate education for naval officers dates back to the 1800s, when USNA engineers were sent abroad to earn graduate degrees. In the early 1900s, when the Navy tried to set up additional service schools for its officers, it faced the trade-off between meeting its short-term operational needs and the long-term benefits of a better-educated officer corps (Powell, 2004). A similar issue remains today: The Navy must determine the optimal level of officer graduate education to meet required capabilities given finite resources in terms of officer end-strength and graduate education funding.

The Navy's primary goal in offering funded graduate education to its officer corps is to "support requirements for officers with specific subspecialty skills" (OPNAVINST 1520.23B, 1991). Thus, the Navy manages its education programs through an integrated manpower and personnel classification system that uses subspecialty codes to identify officer requirements for advanced education, functional training, and significant experience in various fields and positions. The subspecialty code identifies billets requiring specific qualifications and also identifies officers who possess specific qualifications. The code itself has five characters. The first four characters are numbers that identify disciplines (e.g., functional areas and concentrations and educational specialization) needed for a particular billet, while the fifth character is a letter that indicates the level of training, education, or experience needed.

For the purposes, of this study we focused on P- and Q-coded subspecialty designators. Officers having a funded master's degree and billets that require a master's degree carry P-coded designators.[1] Officers who have served in a P-coded billet may receive a Q-code designator, which indicates a "proven subspecialist," meaning that the officer has both a master's degree and experience in his or her subspecialty. A Q-code qualifies the officer to serve in a Q-coded billet. The formal definitions for P and Q codes are as follows (U.S. Navy, 2010, pp. B-11, B-12):

- **P code:** Requires extensive knowledge of theories, principles, processes, and/or techniques certified through the acquisition of the master's degree for optimum performance of duty; also requires the conception, implementation, appraisal, or management of complex Navy and/or DoD programs
- **Q code:** All P-coded criteria are applicable; *additionally* the billet requires the combination of both professional experience and proven subspecialist at the master's degree level.

Officers are considered *funded* if they attend graduate school full time for 26 weeks or more, regardless of whether the degree program is partially or fully funded. For a *fully funded program*, the Navy provides full pay and benefits for the duration of the course of study plus all tuition costs. For a *partially funded program*, the Navy supplies only pay and benefits, and the individual or an organization other than the Navy pays the tuition. An officer will typically only receive one funded graduate school opportunity in his or her career but may acquire additional unfunded degrees. Voluntary graduate school programs, such as tuition assistance or the Montgomery G.I. Bill, are considered unfunded graduate education. Such military institutions as the NPS, AFIT, and various war colleges and civilian institutions offer funded graduate degree programs. About one-half of the full-time residential programs are undertaken at either NPS or NWC (Moskowitz

---

[1] Officers who complete an unfunded master's degree may submit paperwork to the Bureau of Naval Personnel to add a P-code designator to their personnel file. These officers are available for assignment to P-coded positions but have no utilization requirement. According to interviewees, there may actually be disincentives to reporting unfunded graduate education to the bureau.

et al., 2008). Each fiscal year, the Navy has about 390 funded master's degree quotas (seats) at NPS, 25 at AFIT or other military institutions, and 200 at various civilian institutions.[2] About 550 of these are fully funded, and the rest are for such other programs as partially funded scholarships. Appendix A discusses some of the programs through which naval officers can receive a master's degree in more detail.

By DoD policy, officers who receive funded graduate education incur an active-duty service obligation (ADSO) of three months for every one month of schooling for the first year of schooling. The average graduate degree program lasts approximately 18 months. Navy policy requires a minimum three-year ADSO for a funded master's degree and a maximum five-year obligation for a funded doctorate. This ADSO may be served concurrently with any other obligation.[3]

P- and Q-coded billet requirements establish the demand for naval officers with graduate degrees (Table 3.1). In 2008, approximately 5,960 total P-coded billets and approximately 760 Q-coded billets were available for those in grades O-3 through O-6 (captain). For the purposes of this study, we removed the medical, dental, law, and chaplain billets from the total validated billets, resulting in 4,397 P-coded and 481 Q-coded billets.

Table 3.1
Distribution of Billets Requiring Master's Education, by Grade

Grade	O-3	O-4	O-5	O-6	Total
Total authorizations (P and Q codes)	1,720	2,129	1,957	915	6,721
Authorizations without medical, dental, chaplain, and law	1,127	1,529	1,513	709	4,878

SOURCE: Data from Defense Manpower Data Center, 2008.

---

[2] In Navy terminology, *quota* refers to an individual billet for a training or education course. Navy program managers control a discrete number of quotas for each program, which they can allocate to individuals. Typically, the individual's command will request a quota for a specific program, and the program manager will either approve or disapprove the request.

[3] If the Navy funds an officer for a master's degree through IGE, the officer's ADSO is five years served concurrently with any other service obligations.

We used the number of funded school quotas to determine the supply of officers having graduate degrees. Every year the Navy sends approximately 550 to 600 officers to school to receive advanced degrees. Most officers complete their graduate degrees between grades O-3 (lieutenant) and O-4; historically these two grades have accounted for 70 to 80 percent of all graduate degrees attained per year (Moskowitz et al., 2008). As of 2009, approximately 12,150 naval officers in grades O-3 and O-6 had master's degrees, as designated by either a P-code (8,956) or Q-code (3,194).[4] These are the officers available for utilization in billets requiring graduate degrees. However, the number of officers who have had *funded* graduate education in 2009 was 6,683. Policy only requires funded officers to serve a utilization tour.

DoD utilization policy for officers who have had funded graduate education—which was modified in 2008—states that officers should be assigned to a P-coded position as soon as possible following degree completion and, ideally, immediately after.[5] The current Navy policy (OPNAVINST 1520.23B) has not been revised since 1991 and states that

> Officers who have received funded graduate education will serve one tour in a validated subspecialty position as soon as possible but not later than the second tour following graduation.

In practice, the "second tour following graduation" has been interpreted as the second *shore* tour following graduation to account for operational requirements, which often preclude URL officers from immediate utilization in validated billets.

Navy education program managers currently use the one-tour officer utilization metric to evaluate and report on the effectiveness of master's degree programs. Program managers track the percentage of officers who serve in a validated billet within one shore tour after

---

4   This includes all staff, URL, and RL officers but excludes limited-duty officers and chief warrant officers.

5   There is no utilization requirement for unfunded education.

receiving their degrees and within their careers. A qualifying utilization tour typically lasts from two to three years and varies by Navy community.

Given the number of Q-coded officers in the Navy in 2009, we can assume that 26 percent of all graduate-educated officers currently in the Navy between grades O-3 and O-6 have completed at least one utilization tour. The Navy reports that 23 percent of officers complete one utilization tour within two shore tours following graduation. The estimated average career assignment rate for active-duty officers to utilization billets across the entire Navy is 53 percent, while URL and RL assignment rates are between 47 and 73 percent, respectively.[6] Rates also vary by community; for example, oceanography and civil engineering have the highest career utilization rates, while aviation and special operations have the lowest.

While approximately 86 percent of all P- or Q-coded billets that require master's degrees are filled, the officers who fill them do not necessarily have graduate degrees or degrees specific to the billet requirements (Education Coordination Council, 2010). The efficiency of the subspecialty billet program is evaluated in terms of exact fits, exact matches of billet and officer subspecialty codes, and matrix fits, close matches of billet and officer subspecialty codes.[7] The estimated average matrix fit rate for all communities is about 35 percent; the exact fit rate is lower, only about 24 percent. Again, the URL community performs poorly in matching graduate degrees to billet requirements, with 15 percent being exact fits, while 21 percent are exact fits in the RL community.[8]

---

[6] This figure may overstate career assignment rates because the data exclude officers who have received a graduate education and have left the Navy without completing a utilization tour.

[7] In a matrix match, the first one or two numbers of the subspecialty code are the same for the billet and the officer, but the other numbers might not match. For instance, a billet designated 2000 for "National Security Studies—General" might be filled with an officer with the subspecialty 2400P for Strategic Intelligence.

[8] The relative efficiency of the URL communities in exact fits to billets may be due to differences in billet coding practices between the URL and RL communities; evaluating these

Service Comparisons

Marine Corps Graduate Education Program

The Marine Corps has two funded graduate education programs. The largest, which is fully funded and accounts for more than one-half the service's annual quotas, is the Special Education Program (SEP) set out in Marine Corps Order (MCO) 1520.9G. Officers in the SEP program may attend NPS, AFIT, or accredited civilian universities.[9] The other program, set out in MCO 1560.19E, is the Advanced Degree Program, which is intended to augment the SEP by partially funding degrees at civilian institutions.[10] Specific quotas for various curricula at particular schools are based on requirements projected three years in advance. Officers who are accepted and enroll in a graduate education program incur an ADSO of three YOS for the first year of school and four YOS for schooling that lasts more than one calendar year. The ADSO is concurrent with any other service obligation.

With the exception of degrees awarded at staff colleges, all graduate degrees are awarded at grades O-1 (second lieutenant) through O-4 (major). Although this rank limitation exists, there are no time-in-service limitations for graduate education. Officers must apply to a graduate education selection board, and the annual admission process is competitive. The board evaluates and selects officers based on "career potential, past performance of duty, previous academic record, and availability for assignment" (MCO 1520.9G, 2003). Officers are asked to list their top five degree curricula and are paired with degree programs based on program availability, aptitude, and military occupational specialty (MOS) requirements. Upon graduation, the officer is assigned an additional MOS (AMOS). Officers are encouraged to align

---

differences would require a detailed analysis of billet coding, which was beyond the scope of this research.

[9]   Officers must be accepted by the civilian institution, and the curriculum should be one that is not readily available at either NPS or AFIT.

[10]   Officers are responsible for their own tuition, books, and fees but receive all their regular pay and benefits while at school.

their degree programs with their primary MOS to stay close to their career paths during their utilization assignments.

The Marine Corps funds approximately 180 annual graduate education quotas to fill approximately 385 billets. An officer who is eight to ten months out from graduation will receive orders for a follow-on utilization tour in a validated billet. The Marine Corps SEP policy recognizes the particular challenges career-path restrictions aviators face in completing utilization tours. Because graduate education and utilization tours can take aviators out of the cockpit for up to five years (a combination of the length of the graduate course and the utilization tour), the SEP instruction requires aviators to meet their first "flight gate" before applying to SEP.[11] On completing a utilization tour, Marine Corps officers retain the AMOS and are monitored for possible subsequent assignments to utilization tours; however, subsequent tours are rare (Blair, 2009).

The Marine Corps philosophy toward graduate education is to develop skills that fulfill immediate and specific requirements. In FY 2009, 385 Marine Corps billets required graduate educations. Officers are expected to serve a three-year utilization tour immediately after graduating. The Marine Corps defines *utilization* as work that exactly or closely matches the officer's AMOS and the billet's AMOS requirement. According to program managers, officers are assigned to billets that do not exactly or closely match their AMOSs less than 1 percent of the time. In 2009, the Marine Corps reported a 96-percent utilization rate for officers in their first tours following graduate education, the highest utilization rate for any of the services for which researchers had accurate figures (Blair, 2009).

Air Force Graduate Education Program

The Air Force view of graduate education is more consistent with the new DoD instruction than that of the Marine Corps. The general philosophy is that graduate education gives officers critical thinking skills

---

[11] The first flight gate is defined as six years of operational flying in the first ten years of service. Provided the first flight gate is met, aviation incentive pay will continue through graduate school and in the follow-on utilization billet.

that are used every day in an officer's job, regardless of billet requirements. The Air Force describes graduate education programs as helping to manage resources and support objectives in "an increasingly complex international environment with rapidly changing science and technology" (Air Force Instruction 36-2302, 2001). The Air Force provides advanced academic degree (AAD) funding to "prepare officers to perform the duties of a specifically designated position (or to meet the needs of a particular career field)" (Air Force Policy Directive 36-23, 1993).

The annual graduate school quota is about 460 per year, given funding availability and student man-year (end-strength) limitations. Funded graduate opportunities are available at AFIT, intermediate service colleges, war colleges, and a variety of civilian institutions.[12] Officers typically attend graduate school at the O-3 and O-4 levels but may have up to three or four funded degrees throughout their careers.[13] Graduate education is a factor in promotion boards, and 98 percent of officers selected for promotion at their O-5 (lieutenant colonel) boards have graduate degrees. Officers may also have more than one funded degree in their career paths, including a doctorate or programs at war colleges and intermediate service colleges.

Officer selection is based on the "best available" officer, that is, the officer with the right background and aptitude who is at the right point in his or her career track. Typically, the officer's senior rater nominates the service member, then the development team for the career field evaluates and steers him or her into an available program following "best fit" criteria. Funded master's programs typically last two years, while doctoral programs typically take five years. The ADSO for an officer receiving funded education is three years for a master's degree and five years for a doctorate.

---

[12] Graduate degrees at civilian institutions are sponsored by AFIT and are generally approved only if there is no comparable curriculum at AFIT.

[13] Pilots tend to have different career timing and graduate school opportunities because of the pressures to keep them in the cockpit and to get an ROI for their pilot training.

After graduation, the officer is assigned a P code for a master's degree or an R code for a doctorate.[14] Career-field managers validate billets that require graduate education every year, and the subspecialty areas depend on the current priorities of the Air Force. Air Force officers who have had funded graduate education are required to serve in a validated billet within two assignments following graduation. By directive, the Air Force uses two metrics to evaluate compliance with graduate education policy annually:

1. the percentage of AFIT-produced degrees (master's and doctorate) as a fraction of the number of AAD billet requirements
2. the percentage of AFIT graduates assigned to AAD billets within two assignments following graduation.

In its 2008 biennial review of graduate programs, the Air Force reported that 59 percent of officers who had received a funded graduate degree between FY 2006 and FY 2008 had been assigned to an AAD billet within their first two assignments following graduation. The remaining 41 percent, who had not been assigned to an AAD position, were still in their first assignments following graduation and were expected to fill AAD positions in their next assignments. The Air Force also reported an additional metric in this review, an evaluation of whether the individuals who were not assigned to an AAD billet in their first assignments used their graduate educations in the non-AAD billets. This analysis was subjective and based on a comparison of the observed billet requirements with the degree curricula. The Air Force reported that 31 percent of officers in non-AAD assignments immediately following graduation were in positions that utilized their AAD skills.

Army Graduate Education Programs

The Army considers higher education to be both something of a sabbatical from operational responsibilities and a broadening experience.

---

[14] Professional degrees, such as legal or medical doctorates, receive an "S" code. A list of data codes can be found in Air Force Instruction 36-2305.

GEN David Petraeus elaborated six reasons that he believed graduate education (at civilian universities in particular) was important to the Army (Petraeus, 2007):

- It took military officers out of their intellectual comfort zones, which is critical in developing adaptable and creative leaders.
- It exposed them to different viewpoints and cultures.
- It provided general intellectual capital.
- It helped officers develop and refine communication skills.
- It helped officers improve critical thinking skills.
- It imparted intellectual humility and helps raise individual standards of excellence.

The Army currently runs two separate graduate education programs. The first, the Advanced Civil Schooling program, focuses on meeting validated billet requirements. The program funds approximately 412 graduate education quotas annually to fill about 2,000 validated billets.[15] The Army stratifies these quotas by low-, medium-, and high-cost universities and will pay up to $45,000 in total tuition for high-cost universities, such as Harvard or Stanford.[16] The Army tries to select "quality" officers for the Advanced Civil Schooling program and, in particular, tries to send high-performing, high-aptitude officers to elite universities.

The second program was started to provide retention incentives to Army officers who have seen higher operational tempos and increasing deployment-to-dwell ratios in recent years because of the conflicts in Iraq and Afghanistan. The Expanded Graduate School Program currently funds 200 to 400 quotas and is expected to have funding for as many as 600 by 2012. Graduates of this program may elect to do a degree from a broader range of curricula and institutions and are not required to complete a utilization assignment; however, they are required to complete an ADSO.

---

[15] In the past, the Army has had up to 5,300 validated billets.

[16] This is in addition to the programming rate for each officer which includes full pay and benefits.

The Army has the longest ADSOs of any of the services. Officers who receive funded graduate education are required to serve three months of active-duty for every one month of education. This requirement means that the typical two-year master's degree incurs an ADSO of six years following graduation.

Like the other services, the Army also looks at utilization rates to evaluate the performance of its funded education programs.[17] Officers' records are flagged as soon as they receive a funded degree, and the assignment officer is required to check with the utilization manager for follow-on assignments before the flag can be removed from the officer's record. The metric for measuring performance in the Expanded Graduate School Program is simply retention rates.

Cross-Service Program Parameters and Management

Table 3.2 compares advanced academic programs and billet requirements across the services, showing that, proportionally, the Navy has more billets requiring officers with graduate degrees than the other services do. In fact, relative to the overall size of the officer corps, the Navy, with approximately 5,000 billets and 25,600 officers, requires about three times as many as the Army or Air Force and nearly nine times as many as the Marine Corps.[18]

Again relative to the size of its officer corps, the Navy also has more quotas for graduate education than the other services do. However, these quotas are not proportionate to the billet requirements. Every year, the Navy has one quota for about every nine validated billets. The Army has one for every five validated billets, the Air Force one for every six, and the Marine Corps one for every two. Given the

---

[17] The Army was not able to provide us information on utilization rates from its most recent biennial review of graduate education programs.

[18] It is unclear whether the high number of billets requiring graduate education in the Navy relative to other services is due to additional technical requirements in the Navy or whether the billet validation criteria for graduate education differ substantially between the services. This would require a detailed analysis of billet validation procedures, which was beyond the scope of this research but would be a valuable area for further research.

Table 3.2
Cross-Service Comparisons

	Navy	Air Force	Army	Marine Corps
Active-duty service obligation	Master's, 3 years PhD, 5 years	Master's, 3 years; PhD, 5 years	3 years for each year of study[a]	3 years for 1 year of study; 4 years for >1 year
Size of officer corps, O-3 to O-6[b]	25,600	37,900	36,600	11,620
Annual graduate education quota	~550	~460	~400[d] +200[e]	~180
Quota-to-billet requirement ratio	1:9	1:6	1:5	1:2
Billet requirements, O-3 to O-6	~5,000[c]	~2,600	~2,050	~385
Percentage of all billets	20	7	6	3
Officer utilization rates (%)	23[f]	59[g]	Data unavailable	96[g,h]
Measures of program effectiveness	Utilization in two shore tours over a career	Utilization in first or second assignment	Utilization and retention	Utilization and reutilization

[a] A two-year degree would then mean a six-year ADSO.
[b] This number excludes all officers in medical, law, and chaplain specialties.
[c] Approximate number of P's and Q's.
[d] Advanced civil schooling.
[e] Expanded Graduate School Program.
[f] In two shore tours. These data are from the Navy's Biennial Review of Graduate Education Programs dated December 10, 2008.
[g] In the first assignment.
[h] The Marine Corps reports this as an "exact fit" with degree and billet assignment.

potential availability of eight billets to every officer in the Navy who has a new graduate degree, officer utilization rates could be expected to be very high. However, the one-tour utilization rate in the Navy is less than 25 percent within two tours after graduation and an average of 51 percent over a career. These are the lowest rates among the services for which utilization data were available.

The cross-service comparison suggests that, while all the services educate to fill validated billets, slight variations occur in services' overall philosophy toward graduate education. In addition, there are considerable differences in program management and program parameters between the Navy's graduate education program and those of the other services. Chapter Four explores program parameters and utilization management within the Navy in more detail.

Community-Level Data and Utilization Model

Not only do the services differ from one another in how they manage their graduate education programs, but the various communities within the Navy have differences from one another. Community managers and education program managers have highlighted their philosophical differences about graduate education and the billet structure and utilization rates among the URL, RL, and staff corps communities.

URL officers in the Navy are officers who are qualified to command operational units, ships, or aviation squadrons and include surface warfare, submarine warfare, aviation, and special warfare communities. RL officers, such as information professionals, information warfare officers, and naval oceanographers, are not eligible for command at sea. Career opportunities, including educational and utilization opportunities, are thought to differ between URL and RL communities because of the extra position requirements (career wickets) necessary for operational commands in URL communities.

We explored these differences further by developing a system dynamics leader succession model to improve our understanding of how officer assignment decisions and career management affect utilization rates among various communities. This model starts with a pool of graduate-degreed officers and makes certain assumptions about how these officers progress though their careers, including promotion and retention rates up to grade O-5 (commander).[1] Although the model could be modified for any Navy community, we selected one repre-

---

[1] See Appendix C for more details.

sentative community from the RL and one from the URL: the surface warfare officer (SWO) community for the URL community and the meteorology and oceanography (METOC) for the RL community.[2]

Community Differences

Surface Warfare Community

SWOs are required to complete four sea tours (two tours as a division officer and two as a department head) within their first 10 to 12 YOS, three of which are expected to be in mainstream afloat billets.[3] With these operational demands, individuals in the SWO community typically have one opportunity to attend graduate school in their first ten YOS, during their first shore tour at 4 to 6 YOS and grade O-3. A very small percentage of officers may complete their graduate schooling earlier through the VGEP or IGE program, and some may not complete graduate education until they attend NWC at higher grades. Approximately 90 to 100 funded graduate education quotas are available to the SWO community every year.

Subspecialty requirements in the SWO community fall into five broad categories and 29 subcategories. The subspecialty areas having the most billet requirements are listed in Table 4.1. A majority of the billet requirements in this community are for technical subspecialties that are closely related to operational roles. In URL communities, master's level and higher education requirements are not normally applied to shore duty billets for grades below O-4.[4]

Retention has been a frequent concern for the SWO community. Retention rates are typically measured at 7 to 9 YOS and have mainly fluctuated between 30 and 40 percent in the past decade (Lorio, 2006).

---

[2] The METOC community is also sometimes called the OCEANO (for oceanography) community.

[3] See Moskowitz et al., 2009, for more on the operational demands SWOs face.

[4] See U.S. Navy, 2010. Shore-duty billets below the O-4 level might benefit from advanced degrees; however, these billets are not likely to be designated for officers with graduate educations because the timing of degree attainment in the URL communities precludes most officers from being available to fill these billets before grade O-4.

Table 4.1
Top Five Subspecialty Requirements in the
SWO Community

Subspecialty Area	Code	Total P and Q Billets
Undersea warfare	6301	88
Combat systems	5700	54
Plant propulsion	5203	44
General engineering and technology	5000	43
General operations	6000	39
Total		268

SWOs incur an ADSO for graduate education, which is the same as for other communities. However, assignments to some graduate degree programs also require SWOs to sign up for SWO Continuation Pay, which is designed as a retention incentive and awards officers up to $50,000 to stay in the SWO community and complete two operational department-head tours with a deployable unit. Together, these two sea tours typically last five to six years, including training and the time involved in changing duty stations. Thus, an SWO who agrees to attend graduate school is actually more likely to have a minimum five-year commitment to active service following his or her graduation.[5] Therefore, retention rates at the 7- to 9-year point for SWOs who have had graduate degrees may be artificially higher than those for officers without graduate degrees and are thus not necessarily accurate representations of the effect of graduate education on retention.

Promotion incentives in the SWO community are not currently aligned to encourage graduate degree attainment or utilization. Although the SWO community has begun to track promotion statistics for officers who have graduate degrees, master's degree attainment or utilization in a validated billet is not a required criterion for promotion at any grade. Community managers suggested that promotion is

---

[5]   In the case of the SWO community, the "unofficial" ADSO is similar to the Army's official ADSO for graduate education.

primarily based on performance in operational billets and, at most, a
graduate degree on an officer's record might be a "tie-breaker" in the
promotion board, given two officers with similar promotion potential
in all other respects.

The SWO community in 2008 had a total of 385 P-coded billet
and 49 Q-coded billets out of 4,485 total SWO billets between grades
O-3 and O-6; thus, billets requiring a master's level of education
accounted for fewer than 10 percent of all SWO billets.[6] As Figure 4.1
shows, the distribution of P and Q billets increases at higher grades,
and these billets account for 37 percent of all billets at the O-6 level
compared with only 2.5 percent of billets at the O-3 level. This distribution of billets suggests that this community has proportionally

Figure 4.1
Distribution of P- and Q-Coded Billets for Unrestricted Line Officers
Qualified in Surface Warfare (111x)

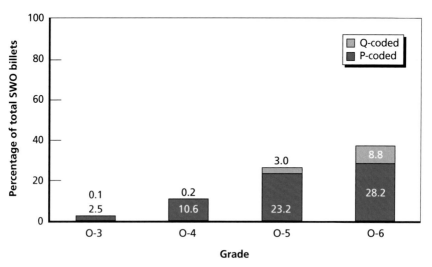

SOURCE: Data from Defense Manpower Data Center, 2008.
RAND MG995-4.1

---

[6] The SWO detailer is responsible for filling a set number of discrete 1110-coded (SWO)
validated billets, as well as a "fair distribution" of nondiscrete 1050- and 1000-coded (any
URL) validated billets. For the purpose of this research, we calculated billet numbers for
SWO-designated billets only.

greater requirements for graduate degrees and proven subspecialists at the higher grades.

METOC Community

The METOC community has designated specialty discipline areas in three main categories—physical oceanographers, meteorologists, and generalists—which are further subdivided into 12 subdisciplines. Initially, officers are expected to choose a prime specialty area (meteorology or oceanography) and then gain strong expertise in a subdiscipline throughout their careers.

A majority of officers entering the METOC community are selected into the program before commissioning but are actually commissioned as unqualified SWOs and must first fulfill an initial SWO division officer tour. Upon qualification as an SWO, they are automatically redesignated into the METOC community. The METOC community also accepts officers who laterally transfer from other communities, and there are a limited number of officers who are directly commissioned into the METOC community. The first SWO tour is followed by an initial METOC experience tour, which helps the officer understand the METOC community and select a discipline area. At about six to nine years into their careers, METOC officers are expected to complete an education tour—a two-year course of study leading to a master's degree in physical oceanography and meteorology. Most of these degrees are completed at NPS, although a select few (typically one per year) complete their degrees through the Massachusetts Institute of Technology–Woods Hole Oceanographic Institute Joint Program in Oceanography. Each officer is strongly encouraged to choose a thesis topic in his or her preferred subdiscipline.

Officers receiving funded education are expected to do a payback tour in a coded billet. However, the first tour immediately following the education tour is an out-of-community operational tour, sometimes known as an "O-4 sea tour." After this initial tour, officers are encouraged to pursue their discipline track throughout the remainder of their careers, culminating in an O-5 milestone tour, which again utilizes their specialized experience.

The METOC community's philosophy is that "all career officers will attend postgraduate education and obtain a master's degree."[7] In addition, in terms of promotion potential, service in a P-coded billet is considered "necessary, but not sufficient to select to O-5."[8] The billet structure and distribution for the METOC community reflect this emphasis on graduate education. The METOC community has a total of 135 P-coded and 106 Q-coded billet requirements, accounting for 65 percent of the total billet requirements. As Figure 4.2 shows, over one-half the billets at every grade require a master's degree, and at grades O-5 and O-6, over one-half of all billets require a proven subspecialist. The high percentage of billets requiring proven subspecialists suggests a need to reuse officers in validated billets throughout their career.

Figure 4.2
Distribution of P- and Q-Coded Billets for Restricted Line Officers Qualified in Special Duty Oceanography (180x)

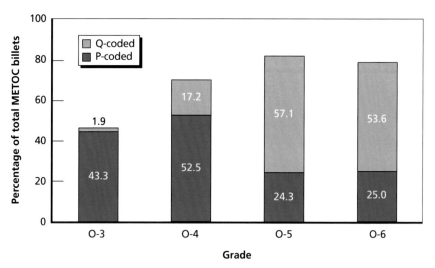

SOURCE: Data from Defense Manpower Data Center, 2008.
RAND MG995-4.2

---

[7]   Navy Personnel Command website, OCEANO detailer's pages.

[8]   Navy Personnel Command website.

Utilization Scenarios Lead to Different Outcomes for Communities

Researchers built a system dynamics leader succession model to test different utilization scenarios in the two communities. We used figures from the Navy's model for graduate school quotas and also made various assumptions about career progression and timing of graduation and utilization tours.[9] In accordance with Navy policy, the researchers assumed that utilization tours would occur at the first opportunity following graduation. Initial model runs examined utilization possibilities given different retention rates for the SWO and METOC communities.

Table 4.2 shows outputs from various model runs in the SWO community. We examined retention rates at 40, 65, and 95 percent. We chose 40 percent as it was the upper bound of average retention rates for this community from the past decade and a maximum retention rate of 95 percent, which would be consistent with retention rates seen in some of the RL communities to make comparisons between communities. However, a 65-percent retention rate would be most realistic for the SWO community, in line with the literature estimations that graduate education improves retention by about 25 percentage points.

In the SWO community, one tour in a utilization billet in an officer's career was sufficient to fill all SWO-only, P-coded billets at the O-3 and O-4 level, even at retention rates lower than 50 percent at seven to ten years. However, with nearly perfect retention rates at seven to ten years and only one utilization tour per career, less than 15 percent of the O-5 P-coded billets can be filled by officers with graduate degrees. If officers complete two or more utilization tours during a career, it becomes possible to fill all the O-5 P-coded billets, given the quotas and billets. Therefore, for the SWO community, the available quotas for graduate education and the billet structure are currently such that at least some officers must complete more than one utilization tour *within a career* for all the P-coded billets to be filled by officers having master's degrees. Because most officers receive funded

---

[9]   See Appendix C for complete model assumptions and limitations.

Table 4.2
Utilization Scenarios in the SWO Community (percent)

| Retention at 7–10 YOS | Grade | Career Utilizations | | |
		One	Two	More than two
95	O-3	100	100	100
	O-4	100	100	100
	O-5	11	83	100[a]
	Total[b]	54	91	100
65	O-3	100	100	100
	O-4	100	100	100
	O-5	3	57	100[a]
	Total[b]	48	78	100
40	O-3	100	100	100
	O-4	94	100	100
	O-5	0	25	100[a]
	Total[b]	46	61	100

[a] Might require more than one utilization in grade.
[b] Assumes 91 SWO graduate education quotas are funded annually.

education at grade O-3, utilization possibilities at the O-5 level (which has the highest proportion of billets) are sensitive to retention rates. However, as Table 4.2 shows, the effects of improved retention on the SWO community's ability to fill billets are small compared to those of reutilization. For example, increasing retention from 40 to 95 percent at seven to ten years increases the percentage of billets filled by only 6 percent (46 to 54 percent); a second utilization tour increases fill possibilities by 30 to 70 percent depending on the retention rates used.

Model runs for the METOC community paint a somewhat different picture than those for the SWO community. The METOC community does not have the same retention issues as the SWO community, so we assumed a 95 percent retention rate. A single utilization tour in a METOC officer's career leaves barely enough school quotas to fill the O-3 billet requirements (even with high retention). Given the model parameters, it was not possible to fill all the requirements in this community without utilizing officers in subspecialty-coded billets at least once in every grade. The percentages in Table 4.3 also do not reflect the Q-coded billet requirements, which are substantial in grades O-5 and O-6. If we added Q-coded billets into the model, it is likely that officers who have had graduate degrees would have to complete more than one utilization tour *at every grade* to fill all the requirements.

The results from this utilization model highlight the importance of career management for officers who have graduate degrees and of reutilization of officers with subspecialties. If officers who have graduate degrees are expected to complete only one utilization tour in a career, the SWO community would need more than double its current school quota to 190 slots to fill all the P-coded requirements in grades O-3 to O-5. The number of annual quotas the METOC community would need to fill requirements would almost triple, to 42, if each graduate-educated officer completed only one utilization tour.[10] This revised quota requirement would be substantial given that there are only about 96 officers at grade O-3 in the METOC community. The next chap-

Table 4.3
Utilization Scenarios in the METOC Community (percent)

Retention at 7–10 YOS	Grade	Career Utilizations			
		One	Two	One at every grade	More than two
95	O-3	100	100	100	100
	O-4	100	100	60	100
	O-5	11	83	100	100[a]
	Total[b]	54	91	79	100

[a] Might require more than one utilization in grade.
[b] Assumes 15 METOC graduate education quotas are funded annually.

---

[10] These estimations assume 95-percent retention rates.

ter includes a further discussion of the billet and educational quota structure for these two communities and their implications for ROI estimations.

CHAPTER FIVE

A Return-on-Investment Framework

Using the data and modeling results from Chapter Four and assumptions drawn from the military and civilian literature review, this chapter uses an ROI framework to analyze the benefits from funding graduate education. The underlying concept is straightforward: trading a one-time initial cost for providing education for a future benefit of needed knowledge for service in particular billets and available skills for service in all future billets. The **costs** are providing a billet for education for each officer for one to two years, paying tuition or substituting a proxy value for tuition when it is not paid directly. The **benefits** accrue from increased officer productivity due to the knowledge and skills gained and from filling billets that require this knowledge and these skills. It is not likely that a "cash-on-cash" return is achievable or measurable. In the detailed assessment below, we indicate when budget savings might be achievable in future years, but it is an "economic" return that is actually assessed.

Aside from the individual investment, the annual cost overall needs to be taken into account. Given 550 new quotas each year for about 1.5 years of graduate education, the program requires a total annual investment of approximately $135 million. Furthermore, the billet management program, which handles approximately 4,500 P-coded billets and 500 Q-coded billets, is a $940 million annual investment in productivity ("readiness) that should be considered separately. Each of these is discussed below.

Return on the Investment in Education

Variables Included

The variables that make up an ROI framework are outlined below. The analysis could be done for the Navy as a whole, separately for Navy URL and RL, or separately for a particular community. The data for URL and RL combined are presented below, and following that are examples for particular communities.

- Inputs and Intermediate Calculations
  - *Number of graduate education billets to be filled.* For URL and RL, approximately 4,500 billets require graduate degrees, and another 500 require graduate degrees and experience. These are the P- and Q-coded billets described earlier.
  - *Annual quotas for graduate education.* There are 550 quotas each year.
  - *Length of education.* The average is estimated between 1.5 years to 1.8 years. We used the lower bound of 1.5 years for our calculations, but this figure is easily modified in the analysis. This average and the number of annual graduate education quotas are key determinants of cost because a 1.5-year average for 550 new quotas each year translates into the equivalent of 825 annual school seats or billets that must be funded. A 1.8-year average would yield about 990 school seats to fund annually.
  - *Cost of one year of education.* The typical student is an O-3, but some O-4s also attend. We used a programming rate for O-3 and O-4, heavily weighted toward O-3, of $140,000 for the cost of a billet in the student portion of the individual's account.[1] To that, we added an annual proxy tuition cost of

---

[1] The Office of the Secretary of Defense publishes the composite standard pay and reimbursement rates for DoD military personnel annually. These provide data for calculating military manpower costs for program submissions and budget/management studies. The annual DoD composite rate, for each military service and enlisted and officer pay grade, includes average basic pay plus retired pay accrual, health accrual, basic allowance for housing, basic allowance for subsistence, incentive and special pay, permanent change of station expenses, and miscellaneous pay. As discussed earlier, we weighted the O-3 and O-4 Navy officer costs appropriately to determine the average cost for a typical billet. See Roth, 2009.

$25,000, for an annual cost of $165,000 each for the number of school seats calculated above. Multiplying the two numbers (825 school billets at an annual cost of $165,000) yields the approximate cost of the education program, $135 million. Also, while the cost of one year of education (billet plus tuition) is $165,000, the cost per officer is about $245,000, assuming the 1.5 years of education.

- *Value of a billet and value of an officer.* The billets of interest (P and Q) are a mix of O-3 to O-6 billets. Weighting annual programming costs by the percentage of each grade in the billets yields an average annual figure of $157,000. We assumed that the amount programmed for the billet is the value of both the billet and the officer who fills it.[2]

- *Value of a billet requiring a graduate degree.* Assuming a 20-percent productivity gain from graduate education,[3] the value of a billet requiring a graduate degree is $188,000. The total value of all billets is thus $850 million for the 4,500 P-coded billets and an additional $90 million for the 500 Q-coded billets, for a total value of $940 million.

• Benefits
- *Value of an officer with a graduate degree.* With the assumption of a 20-percent productivity gain, the officer who has a graduate degree provides $188,000 of annual value while serving in a billet requiring graduate education, or $31,000 more in value than an officer in that billet without graduate education.[4] This annual value is applied to the number of YOS in the billet, which we assumed to be three. Longer service provides more

---

[2] The billet cost is derived from the DoD programming rates discussed earlier. As discussed in the literature review, economic returns of education are measured in the private sector through earnings differentials. Presumably, a rational firm pays what the person is worth in terms of productivity. We make the similar assumption here.

[3] This assumption is derived from the civilian literature discussed earlier. See Appendix D for an analysis of sensitivity to this assumption.

[4] Our analysis assumed all billets to be manned with an officer either with or without a graduate degree. "Gapped" billets (that is, those not filled by anyone) present issues for the Navy beyond the scope of this analysis.

value. Moreover, we assumed a 5-percent skill productivity differential (about $8,000) for all future billets that were not P or Q coded but in which an officer having a graduate degree might serve.

- *Increased retention.* Simple logic would mandate that officers who have graduate degrees would serve longer on average because their ADSOs following graduation would draw them closer to ten YOS, at which point vesting of retirement at the 20-year mark becomes a dominant consideration. Some of the literature discussed earlier has measured the retention increase, something that the evaluation chapter suggested should be done periodically. The benefit of increased retention is in reducing the annual costs of accessing and training new officers. These savings are potentially significant, as the studies cited described, but are not included in this initial assessment.

- *Reutilization.* The initial benefit described above is for first service in a billet requiring a graduate degree for an average of two years. Any subsequent use in P- or Q-coded billets provides additional annual value without additional cost. If the system were a steady state, any reutilization would also reduce the number of new quotas needed to fill billets, which would provide further savings.

Variables Not Included in the Analysis

A more-complete analysis might make assumptions and include at least two additional variables: depreciation and opportunity costs. Some of the literature discusses knowledge depreciation: the loss of knowledge when it is not used soon after it is gained. However, in our interviews, some indicated that even if not used, an officer educated in a particular field has an interest in staying abreast of that field through journal articles, symposia, etc., so depreciation might not occur. Opportunity costs affect both the officer and the organization. While in graduate school, the officer is forgoing an operational assignment for the same length of time, one that might have provided experience that could have improved his or her promotion potential. The Navy's opportunity costs derive from a possible loss of readiness from the officer being in school instead of an operational billet. It would be necessary to make assumptions about these costs because we are not aware of any studies that have analyzed them.

Also, as discussed above, we assumed longer service, given the graduate degree, but none of the benefits of increased retention, such as lower accession and training costs. We also did not account for the time value of money in this assessment.

Is There a Net Benefit?

Simple math would say that, for the Navy URL and RL, each grad-uate-degreed officer would need to serve an average of about 7.9 YOS in a designated billet to offset the $245,000 total educational cost at $31,000 in added value each year. Obviously, given detailing prac-tices, the likelihood of this would vary by community. Introducing the variables of the skill productivity differential, increased retention, length of education, and reutilization increases the calculated benefit. For example, if at the end of education (at six YOS) an O-3 stays to 20 years and serves in one designated billet for three years and other billets for 11 years, the value (ignoring the time value of money) would be $31,000 for each of the three years plus about $8,000 for each of the other 11 years for a total of $181,000, which is less than the cost of education for 1.5 years of education but greater than the cost of one year of education. If the officer were to be utilized in designated billets twice for three years each, the benefit would be $186,000 plus $48,000 for a total of $230,000, or within 6 percent of the approximate cost of 1.5 years of education. Obviously, in these examples, we assumed that all newly graduated O-3s would stay exactly 20 years. In reality, some would leave earlier, and some would stay longer. Moreover, every officer provided graduate education would have to serve in designated billets for the benefit to accrue across all the URL and RL. An officer who served for 14 additional years after completing graduate education but who never filled a designated billet would provide $112,000 of value, and that is much less than the cost of the education provided. The over-all ROI for the Navy thus depends heavily on the length of education and the usage rate of educated officers in designated billets.[5] Also, as stated above, we are not assessing the considerable savings in accession and training costs if officers who would otherwise have left would stay longer as a result of having been provided graduate education. That analysis is beyond the scope of this study, but Chapter Four outlined how this could be done and incorporated in the analysis.

Effects on Specific Communities

We can use the modeling results from Chapter Four to assess the effects on two communities, SWOs and METOC officers, in more detail. For each, we make the simplifying assumptions of 1.5 years of education, three-year utilization tours, 14 years of additional service after education, $165,000 annual cost to educate (thus a per officer cost of $245,000 for the 1.5 years), a 20-percent knowledge and skill productivity premium while serving in validated billets, and a 5-percent skill productivity premium while serving in other billets.[6] Thus, the cost of education is fixed while, in the figures below, the benefits vary with the level of utilization.

Surface Warfare Officers

Because there are about six times more graduate education quotas for SWO officers (91) than for METOC officers (15), the annual cost to educate them is also six times larger. The break-even point for SWO occurs at about six total years of utilization for every officer provided a graduate education. Any level of utilization above that increases the return on the investment in education. Any level of utilization below that decreases the ROI. Current data show that only about 80 percent of graduate-degreed SWO officers who stay for 20 years serve at least one utilization tour. Many of the officers who do serve in designated billets generally serve in them for less than three years, and the billets

---

[5]   Sending officers to graduate education as early in a career as possible increases payback (potential years of utilization), assuming that the officers are retained.

[6]   All these can be varied in the equations; a sensitivity analysis is included in Appendix D.

often do not match their subspecialties.[7] Given this practice, it is not likely that any scenario would generate an ROI for their education without significant change in management of SWO officers.

Figure 5.1 shows the returns for all SWO officers for three different levels of utilization. Costs are in millions of dollars, representing the cost of the entire SWO community of officers. The Navy breaks even at 100-percent utilization if officers serve two three-year utilization tours. That is to say, to break even, the Navy must have every SWO officer who gets funded graduate education serve two full utilization tours. The break-even point could also occur if only 70 percent of the officers had a utilization tour, but this would require a total of nine years of utilization.

Figure 5.1
Return on Investment: Surface Warfare Officer Community

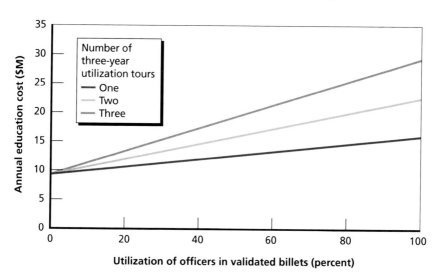

---

[7]   Data from Navy N15 show that, for the Navy overall, about 30 percent of officers with a master's degree and 20 YOS have served in a billet requiring that specific education.

METOC

The costs and benefits for METOC officers have the same relationships as they do for the SWO community but at lower dollar levels because of the lower number of quotas. However, METOC officers generally have high levels of utilization and repeat assignments in validated billets, making an ROI achievable. As shown in Figure 5.2, this break-even return would occur at about six YOS for all officers in designated billets or at nine YOS for about 70 percent of officers.

Figures 5.1 and 5.2 have different y-axes (cost) because one community has more quotas for education than the other community. But they have the same utilization lines because the ROI is independent of the numbers of educational quotas that drive cost. The return is dependent only on the utilization rate and productivity assumption (also given assumptions of completing education at seven YOS and staying to 20 years). That is, for any number of officers provided graduate educations, it takes about six years of use in validated billets to break even.

Figure 5.2
Return on Investment: Meteorology and Oceanography Community

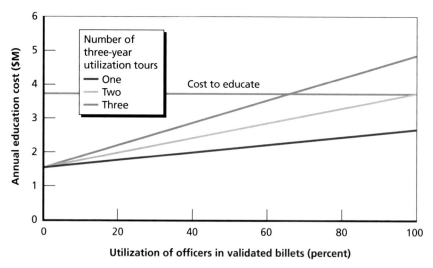

Management of Billets Requiring Graduate Education

Overall, the Navy has about 4,500 P-coded and 500 Q-coded billets that require graduate degrees. Given the weighted grades and composite programming rates of the officers who serve in them, these billets have a readiness or productivity value of $940 million, of which $155 million is the premium for graduate education. Not filling one of these billets at all (gapping it) represents a readiness loss (or an opportunity forgone) of $188,000 for each such billet. If the billet is filled, but with an officer lacking the correct educational credentials, the loss is $31,000 for each such billet.

Current data suggest that, across the Navy, these billets are only accurately filled at about a 36-percent rate, indicating that the Navy is forgoing $109 million of readiness annually.[8] Assuming that the billet requirement is accurate (billets are subject to a zero-based review or validation annually), the Navy would have to either increase utilization significantly or increase quotas for graduate education to reduce the annual productivity loss to zero. There is a trade-off between increasing quotas to reduce the productivity loss and the cost of the additional quotas. Increased utilization in billets is also part of the trade-off, but even with much higher usage, it may not be possible to fill all the designated billets with appropriately educated officers.

From the previous METOC example, we know that six years of utilization in validated billets and seven years of use in other billets of all graduate-educated officers yields a break-even graduate education ROI. However, not all the P and Q billets may be filled at this level of use. The modeling described earlier indicated that more than two utilization tours of three years each would be needed to fill just the P-coded billets. Additional annual quotas would be needed to fill all P and Q billets at this level of use. Alternatively, nine years of utilization for each graduate-degreed officer both increases ROI for the educational benefit

---

8   Data from Navy N15 show that approximately 36 percent of designated billets are filled with officers holding master's degrees that directly or closely align to billet requirements. Thirty-six percent of designated billets are filled by officers that hold master's degrees. Thirty percent of officers have served in a billet requiring a master's degree (from the previous footnote).

and reduces the cost of unfilled billets to near zero. Such levels of utilization might be feasible in this RL community, given the distribution of the Q billets in higher grades.

However, this is not the case for the SWO community. Detailing practices for SWOs would have to change significantly to institute repetitive service and high utilization in validated billets. In essence, SWO officers who have graduate degrees would need to become semispecialized in their subspecialties, which would decrease their opportunities for broadening assignments. Also, because the grade distribution of SWO P and Q billets skews toward O-4 and O-5 ranks, many officers would need to serve in positions one grade below their rank to fill all billets.

The various ratios of graduate education billets to all O-4 to O-6 billets and of quotas for graduation education to P and Q billets tell the tale for both communities. For METOC, 65 percent (213/326) of all billets are coded P or Q, but with 15 quotas, the ratio of billets to quotas is 14 (213/15). This implies that each graduate-degreed officer must serve 14 years of utilization in validated billets to fill all P and Q billets. But this may be feasible, given the high proportion of validated to overall billets and the especially high proportion of 79 percent (22/28) for O-6 billets and 81 percent (57/70) for O-5 P and Q billets to total billets for that grade.

For SWO, only 16 percent (533/3,414) of total billets are P and Q coded, but with 91 quotas, the ratio of billets to quotas is 5.8 (533/91). This implies that each graduate-degreed officer needs to serve slightly less than six years of utilization in a validated billet to have all billets filled. This is a lower rate of utilization than required for an education ROI. It is more likely that the SWOs could fill all designated billets than SWOs could use all officers in a designated billet to generate a return to their educations, but neither is probable with current management practices.

The differences are stark. A high percentage of all METOC billets are P and Q coded. High enough utilization of graduate-degreed officers to achieve an ROI on their education appears feasible. A small percentage of all SWO billets are P and Q coded. Not enough graduate-degreed officers are utilized for a break-even ROI: however, enough are utilized to make filling all validated billets feasible if some SWOs specialize in these billets.

Summary: A Tale of Two Communities

The SWO community educates enough officers to fill validated billets but neither fills the billets completely nor uses officers frequently enough in validated billets to generate a break-even ROI for the education provided. The METOC community uses officers in validated billets frequently enough to generate a return on the investment but, even so, lacks enough quotas to fill all validated billets. Common economic sense would suggest providing more quotas to METOC because in this community the marginal returns exceed the marginal costs.

CHAPTER SIX

Findings and Recommendations

This chapter summarizes the researchers' findings and provides recommendations to the Navy in terms of policy, culture, and monitoring and evaluation.

Findings

The new policy language and intent from the Office of the Secretary of Defense suggest a broader and more-extensive use of funded graduate education beyond educating for validated billets. In particular this is expanded to include educating for "future capabilities." At present, the Navy's graduate education management system and metrics for performance evaluation of that system focus on educating for "present needs." This focus is mainly due to a legacy of a bottom-up approach to managing officer quotas and billets; development of future capabilities implies a top-down process.

Graduate education provides technical skills and nontechnical competencies or "soft skills" which are valued in a wide range of Navy billets beyond billets which require graduate education. Although it is difficult to quantify returns to education, evidence from the literature suggests that positive organizational gains accrue from having a more-educated workforce. Graduate education builds human and social capital that may lead to improved productivity, greater retention, and better performance in billets. Competencies gained in graduate education may compensate for lack of domain knowledge in certain billets.

Cross-service differences exist in graduate education philosophy, program parameters, utilization rates, and particularly in program management. The Navy has one of the largest requirements for graduate education in terms of quotas and validated billets. It also has the lowest utilization rates for officers who have graduate degrees among all the services. Moreover, even if better once-in-a-career utilization rates are achieved, validated billets and graduate school quotas are still mismatched in the Navy; fewer quotas are available than there are validated educational requirements.

Management of officers and billets that require graduate education varies between Navy communities, with pronounced differences between the RL and URL communities. The RL communities have proportionally more billet requirements, more-frequent utilization, and more-frequent reutilization than the URL communities. Cultural influences and career demands within the URL communities often impede demand for graduate school and service in validated billets.

Education execution, billet execution, and officer management are decentralized, and incentives and penalties for managing billets and quotas are not integrated. Community managers and education program managers often have different goals and metrics for assessing program success. Community managers focus on operational issues and gauge their success by how well they fill all the billets in the fleet. Education managers focus on filling graduate school quotas with qualified officers and on placing officers with the proper educational credentials in validated billets. At times these goals clash, with the result being unfilled billets or billets filled by individuals who do not have the requisite experience or qualifications.

The overall benefits in terms of ROI to the Navy from graduate education can be measured given certain assumptions. As Chapter Five indicated, it is possible to make some reasonable assumptions about the costs and benefits of a graduate education. Our approach presents a way to ascertain the costs and make some assumptions to determine benefits. These parameters can be adjusted in the model to identify elements that are particularly sensitive. An order-of-magnitude estimate is quite feasible, and more-precise assessments would be possible with better data.

The current metric, which specifies one utilization per career for each officer with a funded master's degree, as specified DoD and Navy instructions, will not give the Navy a break-even cash ROI within a 20-year career, given our assumptions. Recouping the investment in an officer's graduate education based on skills alone requires long service in billets requiring that education (multiple utilization tours) and even longer service in other billets.

Recommendations

Researcher recommendations are based on the findings of this monograph and cover three areas: policy, culture, and monitoring and evaluation.

Policy

To shift graduate education toward development of future capabilities, the Navy needs to take a top-down approach. Initially, the Navy should review its existing graduate education instructions to verify that the language and intent are aligned with current DoD policy. Recent Navy guidance on graduate education *governance* (OPNAVINST 1520.42, 2009) reflects the new DoD policy more closely than previous versions, but the Navy's overall policy on funded graduate education (OPNAVINST 1520.23B) has not been revised since 1991. Navy policymakers should consider the intent of DoDI 1322.10: "Knowledge is good, and more is preferable." Researchers suggest modifying the existing language of OPNAVINST 1520.23B as outlined in Table 6.1. Once this is complete, Navy leaders need to effectively communicate the resulting policies to graduate education program managers, community managers, and officers.

The cost of graduate education can continue to be justified through service requirements; however, it may take an extremely long time to break even. But if the perceived value of graduate education is the increases in productivity, social capital, and decision quality that

Table 6.1
Recommended Modifications to Navy Graduate Education Policy

Paragraph	Current Policy Language	Recommended Policy Language
3	"Funded graduate education programs **are limited** to providing **sufficient officers** with subspecialties to fill validated billet requirements."	"Funded graduate education programs are offered **to develop a cadre of qualified officers** in areas where advanced proficiency and/or readiness are instrumental to the Navy's current mission or future capability."
4b	"Officers are educated to the graduate level specified by sponsors for optimum performance of duty **in the particular subspecialty area**."	"Officers are educated to the graduate level for optimum performance of duty in **all follow-on assignments** and in particular those assignments requiring the subspecialty designation."
4f(1)	"Officers who have received Navy funded graduate education will serve **one tour** in a validated subspecialty position as soon as possible **but not later than the second tour following graduation**."	"Officers who have received Navy funded graduation will serve **at least one tour** in a validated subspecialty position as soon as possible following graduation."

soft skills and general knowledge offer, the expense becomes an investment in future capabilities, a cost of doing business. If this becomes the
goal, it seems justifiable to make the opportunity for graduate education competitive, targeted toward those most likely to stay in the service and advance to flag rank. In essence, the Navy would be broadly
educating many to achieve future capabilities and an ROI from the
few.

Culture

Increasing emphasis on graduate education as a benefit to the community and to the Navy at large will require a cultural shift for some
Navy communities to overcome negative perceptions associated with
career breaks for education and utilization assignments. In line with a
top-down approach, community leaders need to set goals for graduate
degrees, such as "90 percent of all officers advancing at the O-5 board
will have a graduate degree." In tandem, community leaders need to
develop goals for the types of graduate degree curricula that would sup-

port their anticipated capability requirements beyond current validated billet requirements.

The Navy can take some tactical steps to improve its utilization efficiency immediately by increasing utilization rates and reutilizing officers in validated billets, thus increasing net quantitative ROIs. These steps include incentives for more-integrated management of officer assignments at the community level and penalties for poor management of billets, quotas, and officers. These should vary by community to account for differences in billet structures and operational requirements. One option for penalizing poor management could be cutting graduate education quotas for communities that fail to meet certain threshold utilization rates for officers in validated billets. Community leaders should also seek to provide incentives for matching new graduates with assignments to validated billets to increase economic returns to their education investments. The Navy should consider the Air Force approach, which includes master's degrees in promotion considerations. Officers who are utilized in Q-coded billets increase the Navy's net benefit in terms of ROI; therefore, promotion boards and other incentive initiatives should also give exceptional consideration to "proven subspecialists."

Monitoring and Evaluation

The Navy should expand its utilization metric and enhance monitoring and evaluation of its graduate education program. The one-tour utilization metric needs expansion to account for additional benefits officers with graduate degrees bring the Navy. In particular, when these officers serve in nonvalidated billets, they may offer value that graduate education program managers to not currently capture. We suggest enhancing data collection and periodically evaluating graduate education programs under a hierarchy of outcomes (see Chapter Two). Appendix B offers some specific recommendations on improving data collection and analysis.

Conclusion

The Navy possesses the necessary mix of institutions and curricula in its funded graduate education program to meet its present capability requirements. However, the total value of graduate education to the Navy is not being captured by the metric of one utilization tour as defined in current Navy policy. In fact, given the current timing for graduate school and the typical career progression for officers, one utilization tour per graduate-degreed officer does not recoup the cost of that degree within a 20-year career. We found that both the officer and the Navy benefit from the knowledge and skills graduate education offers. The Navy benefits from the officer's improved productivity, better decisionmaking, and increased retention. Some of this value can be monetized, allowing the costs and benefits to be estimated using enhanced data collection methods and reasonable assumptions. Recent shifts in DoD policy language and intent suggest that the Navy should expand on the one-tour utilization metric to use a more-nuanced assessment of the value of graduate education for the Navy's officer corps, especially with respect to future capabilities.

Master's Degree Opportunities in the Navy

Naval Postgraduate School

NPS, currently located in Monterey, California, began as a postgraduate engineering school for the USNA and became a fully accredited graduate institution in 1955. Its mission is to "provide relevant and unique advanced education and research programs to increase the combat effectiveness of the U.S. and Allied armed forces, and to enhance the security of the United States" (NPS, 2005). It currently supports about 2,000 graduate students enrolled in master's and doctoral programs. At any one time, about one-third of the students come from the U.S. Navy and Naval Reserve, but NPS resident and nonresident programs are available to all service members and to some government civilians and defense contractors. DoD finances the school and its programs directly, along with sponsorship funds.

NPS offers 43 degree programs focusing primarily on engineering, science, technology, national security and business. Out of the 924 degrees awarded in 2008, there were 15 doctorates in engineering, 169 MBAs, 565 master of science degrees, and 175 master of arts degrees. Most naval officers complete a master's degree at NPS as an O-3 during their first shore tour. Officers who are interested in the program must contact their detailers, who will determine whether his or her academic background and professional qualifications are suitable for the desired program. Prospective candidates must have a bachelor's degree from an accredited institution with a grade point average higher than 2.2 on a 4.0 scale.

In 1998, OPNAV estimated total annual military pay (salaries, benefits, and housing) for an NPS-resident officer of $63,300; for a full-time an officer at a civilian institution of $72,300 (Gates et al., 1998). When taking into account program duration and academic fees, OPNAV estimated the total cost of an NPS master's degree to be $231,024, and the weighted average for a selection of 29 civilian institutions naval officers typically attended was $210,112 (Gates et al., 1998).[1]

Immediate Graduate Education

A select number of officers may pursue IGE after completing their undergraduate degrees. Some of these officers will receive partial scholarships, in which the granting organization pays for tuition costs but the Navy pays the officer's full salary, benefits, and housing (if the scholarship does not include housing). Some examples are the Rhodes and Marshall Scholar programs. The Navy also fully funds various IGE programs for officers to allow them to complete their master's degrees at NPS or at a civilian university immediately after commissioning.

For IGE and scholarship programs an officer incurs a service obligation of five years for programs less than 20 months and six years for programs greater than 20 months. This service obligation may be served concurrently with any other service obligations (Harvey, 2006).

VGEP is available to only USNA midshipmen, accommodating up to 20 per year. Students accepted into the program must have validated or completed enough of their coursework by their senior year at the academy to be able to pursue part-time work toward a graduate degree at a nearby civilian university. In addition to being selected by the USNA, the midshipman must also apply to and be accepted by the civilian university's degree program. The student will continue to be assigned to the academy through the duration of the program for administrative purposes and must be able to complete the degree coursework within seven months of graduation from the academy. Authorized fields of study are those that lead to a Navy subspecialty

---

[1]   The most expensive school was estimated to be the California Institute of Technology, at $387,947; the cheapest was the University of Maryland, College Park, at $175,091.

qualification. Costs to the government are up to $10,000 in tuition fees and education expenses, as well as regular in-grade active-duty pay and benefits.

Some officers may be preselected to attend graduate school at the time of their commissioning through the Navy Burke program, which provides deferred opportunities for selected URL officers to obtain graduate degrees in science and engineering fields at NPS. Every year, a select number of USNA, Reserve Officer Training Corps, and Seaman-to-Admiral (STA-21) officer candidates with proven academic performance and leadership potential are chosen for this program prior to commissioning. Unlike the IGE program, the selected officers will first complete a normal operational assignment and will obtain warfare qualification before attending graduate school. During their operational tours, they will need to be in communication with their detailers to discuss their curricula, which is required to be technical.[2]

Burke candidates are required to serve a maximum of three years in their warfare specialty or in a subspecialty utilization tour. Burke candidates who successfully complete their master's programs and have continued high professional performance in their follow-on tours are also eligible to apply for a Navy Burke assignment to a doctoral program.

Politico-Military Master's Program

The Politico-Military program is intended to allow active-duty URL officers to develop a subspecialty in political and affairs and strategic planning through master's degree programs in public policy, security studies, or international relations at highly selective universities.[3] Program duration varies by degree and institution, as shown in Table A.1. Officers in the program are full-time students in duty-under-instruction status. Approximately four quotas are funded for this program annually.

---

[2] If the degree program is not available at NPS the officer may put in a request to attend a civilian university.

[3] These universities include Harvard, Tufts, Johns Hopkins, Stanford, and Georgetown.

All URL officers who have not already completed a funded graduate degree program and are in grades O-3 through O-5 are eligible for the Politico-Military program. Interested officers must apply to the Navy Personnel Command before the Fellowship Program Selection Board convenes in October or November. The board bases its selection on "career performance, academic qualifications, promotion potential, overall fleet requirements, needs of the Navy and overall billets" (OPNAVINST 1500.72F). Officers completing the program will be eligible to receive a 2000P-series subspecialty code, which denotes a master's degree in the area of national security studies.

Table A.1
Politico-Military Master's Programs

University	Degree	Program	Time (years)
Georgetown	MA	Security Studies Program	1
Harvard	MPP	Public Policy	2
	MPA	Public Administration	2
	MPA/ID	Public Administration and International Development	2
	MC/MPA	Midcareer MPA program	1
Johns Hopkins	MA	International Relations	2
	MIPP	International Public Policy	1
Stanford	MA	International Policy Studies	1.5
	MA	International Relations	1.5
Tufts	MALD	Master of Arts in Law and Diplomacy	2
	MA	Fletcher School	1

SOURCE: OPNAVINST 1500.72F, 2007.

Data Collection and Analysis Recommendations

The following are recommended specifications for the personnel file that would be required to conduct a more thorough ROI analysis for funded graduate education in the Navy. The personnel data file should be longitudinal, with observations occurring either on a monthly basis (e.g., active-duty master file) or as transactions take place (e.g., work experience file). The primary variable of interest would indicate that an officer has earned a new master's degree. Most simply, this could be an education variable that changes value from "bachelor's degree" in one observation to "master's degree" in the next. More precisely, a variable indicating the officer's secondary occupation contains, in the fifth position, a letter that takes on the value P or Q if the officer has earned a master's degree.

The following example (Table B.1) illustrates a hypothetical officer who earned a master's degree in March 1993, as shown by both the education and secondary occupation variables. A new transaction is generated every time the officer changes grade, active or reserve component, occupation, or education level. A file with monthly episodes would provide the same level of detail as a transaction-based file like this (which resembles the Work Experience File Database).

Several possible measures could yield information about the Navy's return on investing in an officer's education. The first is YOS after earning a master's degree. In the example above, the officer completes a master's degree in March 1993 and separates from active duty in May 1996, suggesting that the active component of the Navy benefited from the officer's degree for two years and two months. Further,

Table B.1
Sample Individual Work Experience File

Social Security Number	Component	Grade	Occupation				Transaction Date	
			Primary	Duty	Secondary	Education	Beginning	End
123456789	Active	O-2	1310DU	8651	6042	K	12/1/89	2/1/91
123456789	Active	O-3	1310DU	8653	6042	K	2/1/91	9/1/92
123456789	Active	O-3	1310DU	8653	6042	K	9/1/92	3/1/93
123456789	Active	O-3	1310DU	8653	6042P	N	3/1/93	1/1/94
123456789	Active	O-4	1310DU	9085	6040P	N	1/1/94	10/1/95
123456789	Active	O-4	1310DU	9087	6040P	N	10/1/95	2/1/95
123456789	Active	O-4	1310DU	9085	6040P	N	2/1/95	5/1/96
123456789	Reserve	O-4	1310DW	9085	6040P	N	5/1/96	12/1/96
123456789	Reserve	O-4	1310DW	9087	6040P	N	12/1/96	11/1/98
123456789	Reserve	O-5	1310DW	9087	6040P	N	11/1/98	5/1/00

the officer remained in the reserve component from May 1996 to May 2000, and these four years could also be interpreted as part of the ROI. At least three versions of YOS could be considered measures of the return:

- YOS beyond degree award
- YOS beyond ADSO
- career YOS (active-duty and reserve service).

To measure YOS beyond the date the degree was awarded, averages should be computed for those who have earned a master's degree and compared against those who have not. Controls should be based on YOS at the time the degree was completed. So, if the average officer who obtains a master's degree does so after five YOS, the amount of time spent on active duty beyond five YOS is the appropriate measure for those who do not obtain a master's degree.

A similar computation would be done to measure YOS beyond an officer's ADSO and total career YOS. These do not require an initial determination of the starting point for measuring YOS. Rather, the average number of service years beyond ADSO (or total YOS) should simply be compared for those who have earned master's degrees and those who have not. Regardless of the YOS measure, the data could be further disaggregated by such variables as occupation (i.e., compare YOS for oceanographers who have earned a master's degree with those who have not).

A second measure that provides information on the Navy's return from investing in an officer's education is promotion speed. In the data example above, the officer earns a master's degree in March 1993 and is promoted to lieutenant commander in January 1994 after spending two years and 11 months as a lieutenant. Four years and ten months later, he is promoted to commander. To determine whether officers who have earned master's degrees are promoted more quickly than those who have not, the average amount of time spent in each pay grade should be computed for those who have earned master's degrees and compared to those having only bachelor's degrees. The relevant comparisons are the pay grades beyond the officer's rank at the time of degree award. So, for officers who earn a master's degree as a lieutenant, comparisons should be made for the years spent at the ranks of lieutenant commander and above. As with the YOS measures, a finer disaggregation of the data, by occupation, is certainly possible.

Finally, the effectiveness and efficiency of degree utilization provide information on whether investing in an officer's education helps the Navy better match individual skills with billet needs. The data set described above indicates which individuals have P-coded occupations, and this information could be used to determine which billets have been filled by officers having the appropriate skills. Additionally, the secondary occupation code contains information on the officer's subspecialty, as well as details on graduate education ("P" in the fifth position of the field). A computation of the amount of time that passes between graduation and reassignment to a different subspecialty (from 6042 to 6040, ten months after completion of the master's degree in the hypothetical example above) indicates how efficiently the Navy is making use of its new graduate-degreed officers to fill billets.

Model Assumptions and Limitations

We used iThink software to model career progressions for officers with graduate degrees. We started with a pool of school quotas and billets that needed to be filled at each grade from O-3 through O-5. Officers first entered the model at grade O-3, when they started graduate school. From this steady-state stock of graduate-educated officers, we were able to estimate billet fill possibilities at every grade, given certain community-specific assumptions about promotion and tour length. Table C.1 outlines the these assumptions and the model limitations.

Table C.1
Model Assumptions and Limitations

Assumptions	Grade	URL SWO (%)	RL METOC (%)
Timing of master's	O-3	95	95
	O-4	5	5
Duration of master's program		18 months	18 months
Utilization tour length		2 years	3 years
Promotion rates	O-4	0.92	0.90
	O-5	0.90	0.87

NOTES: Utilization occurs at earliest opportunity. Many opportunities exist over a career to utilize graduate education in a P-coded billet.

LIMITATIONS:
1. Addresses general subspecialty fill possibilities not exact subspecialty matches.
2. Does not include Q-coded billets.
3. Excludes officer accessions from other communities (expected to be very small).
4. Does not include officers who received graduate education and subspecialty before O-3 or from unfunded sources.
5. Does not extend beyond O-5.

Return-on-Investment Sensitivity Analysis

For the ROI analysis, we assumed that graduate education supplied a 20-percent productivity gain in validated billets, based on the range of estimated productivity gains that emerged in the literature. The 20-percent gain is actually broken down into two parts: three-fourths (15 percent) of the productivity gain comes from domain knowledge gained in the degree, and one-fourth (5 percent) comes from skills or competencies gained in the course of the education. The 15-percent gain applies only to validated billets, while the 5-percent gain applies to all billets.

The literature estimates a broad range of productivity gains that vary by degree type, institutional quality, and other factors. Therefore, we conducted a sensitivity analysis to examine how varying the productivity rate affects the ROI assessment for funded graduate education in the Navy. We varied our base rate by one-fifth in either direction while keeping the knowledge-to-skill ratio the same to examine total productivity gains at 16 percent (12-percent knowledge and 4-percent skills) and 24 percent (18-percent knowledge and 6-percent skills).

Figure D.1 demonstrates how varying the productivity rates influences the number of years required in validated billets to achieve positive ROIs for graduate education. The ROI break-even point in terms of years of use in validated billets is sensitive to the estimated productivity gain. If we assume a productivity gain of only 16 percent, an officer would need to complete almost nine years (three tours) in validated billets for the Navy to recoup its cash outlay on funded graduate

Figure D.1
Productivity Rate Assumptions Affect Return-on-Investment Possibilities

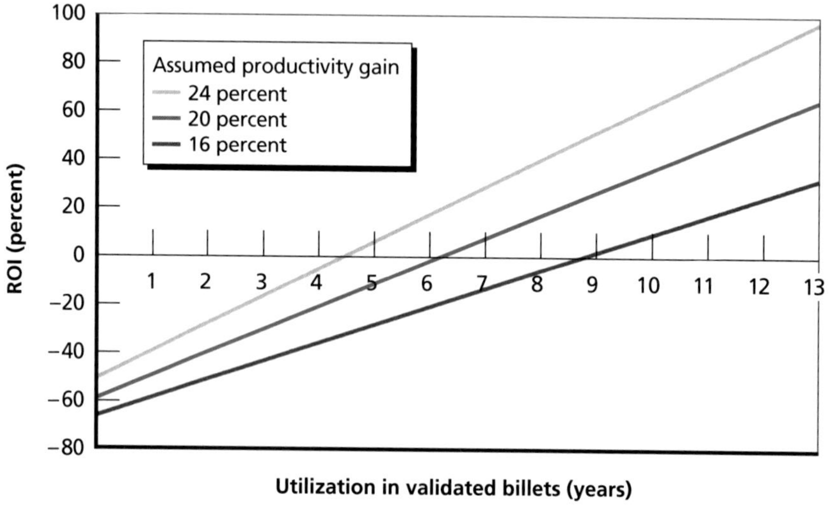

Utilization in validated billets (years)

education. With a 24-percent productivity gain, the officer would need to complete only four years in a validated billet.

Looking at it a different way, we can vary both the number of years the officer spends in utilization billets and the estimated productivity gain to determine the number of YOS required after graduation for the Navy to recoup a cash return on the cost of a master's degree. Table D.1 estimates the YOS and likely rank of the officer at the break-even point for various rates of productivity and years in validated billets. No matter what productivity rate is used within our estimated range, an officer who does only one utilization tour must serve longer than the typical 20-year career for the Navy to see a positive cash ROI for graduate education. In fact, unless we can assume a 24-percent productivity gain, the Navy will not recoup its investment in a 20-year career, even if the officer completes two utilization tours following graduation.

Table D.1
YOS Needed After Degree to Reach Break-Even Point

Years in Validated Billet	Total Productivity Gain (%)	Total YOS Needed	Likely Rank
3	16	30	Senior flag[a]
3	20	23	CAPT
3	24	17	CDR, CAPT
6	16	21	CDR, CAPT
6	20	14	CDR
6	24	8	LCDR
9	16	12	LCDR, CDR
9	20	9[b]	LCDR
9	24	9[b]	LCDR

[a] Given seven YOS at education completion, officer would need to make senior flag rank to stay to 37 YOS.

[b] Staying for a total of 16 years (nine additional years of utilization beyond education) provides a positive ROI.

Bibliography

Air Force Air University, Strategic Leadership Studies, website, undated. As of July 1, 2010:
http://www.au.af.mil/au/awc/awcgate/navy/navy-ldr-comp.htm

Air Force Instruction 36-2302, "Professional Development (Advanced Academic Degrees and Professional Continuing Education)," July 11, 2001.

———, 36-2305, "Education Classification and Coding Procedures," Washington, D.C.: Department of the Air Force, March 1, 2001.

Air Force Policy Directive 36-23, "Military Education," September 27, 1993.

Asch, Beth J., and Warner, John T., *A Theory of Military Compensation and Personnel Policy*, Santa Monica, Calif.: RAND Corporation, MR-439-OSD, 1994. As of June 4, 2010:
http://www.rand.org/pubs/monograph_reports/MR439/

Barno, David W., Lt. Gen. (ret.), and Williamson Murray, testimony before the House Armed Services Subcommittee on Investigation and Oversight, September 10, 2009.

Black, Sandra E., and Lisa M. Lynch, "Human-Capital Investments and Productivity," *The American Economic Review*, Vol. 86, No. 2, May 1996, pp. 263–267.

Blair, A., Biennial Review of Graduate Education Programs, 2009.

Bowman, William R., and Stephan L. Mehay, "Graduate Education and Employee Performance: Evidence from Military Personnel," *Economics of Education Review*, No. 18, 1999, pp. 453–463.

———, "College Quality and Employee Performance: Evidence from Naval Officers," *Industrial and Labor Relations Review*, Vol. 55, No. 4, 2002, pp. 700–714.

Boyatzis, Richard E., E. C. Stubbs, and S. N. Taylor, "Learning Cognitive and Emotional Intelligence Competencies Through Graduate Management Education," *Academy of Management Learning and Education*, Vol. 1, No. 2, 2002, pp. 150–162.

Branigan, Gregory A., *The Effect of Graduate Education on the Retention and Promotion of Marine Corps Officers*, thesis, Monterey, Calif.: Naval Postgraduate School, 2001.

Branstetter, Terry L., Jr., *Measuring the Value of Graduate Information Technology Education for Marine Officers: A Proof of Concept Study*, thesis, Monterey, Calif.: Naval Postgraduate School, 2002.

Brown, Bettina Lankard, "Return on Investment in Training," *Myths and Realities*, No. 16, ERIC Clearinghouse on Adult, Career, and Vocational Education, 2001.

Cashman, Deborah M. Z., *Opinion Survey of Naval Officers Who Have Received a Navy-Sponsored Graduate Degree: A 20-Year Perspective*, thesis, Monterey, Calif.: Naval Postgraduate School, 1994.

Coleman, J. S., "Social Capital in the Creation of Human Capital," *American Journal of Sociology*, No. 94, 1998, pp. S95–S120.

Department of the Air Force Policy Directive 36-23, Military Education, September 27, 1993.

Department of the Army Regulation 621-108, Military Personnel Requirements for Civilian Education, March 26, 2007.

Department of Defense Instruction 26-2302, Professional Development, Advanced Education and Professional Continuing Education, July 11, 2001.

———, 1322.10, Policy on Graduate Education for Military Officers, August 26, 2004.

———, 1322.10, Policy on Graduate Education for Military Officers, April 29, 2008.

Education Coordination Council, VCNO–Directed Navy Strategic Study Review, briefing, March 2, 2010.

Filizetti, Julie, *Master's Degree Highly Desired: Measuring the Increase in Productivity Due to Master's Education in the United States Navy*, PhD thesis, University of Pennsylvania, 2003.

Fitz-Enz, Jac, *How to Measure Human Resources Management*, New York: McGraw-Hill, 1995.

Fitz-Enz, Jac, *The ROI of Human Capital,* New York: American Management Association, 2000.

Fukuyama, Francis, "Social Capital and Development: The Coming Agenda," *SAIS Review*, Vol. 22, No. 1, 2002, pp. 23–37.

Gates, William R., Xavier K. Maruyama, John P. Powers, Richard E. Rosenthal, and Alfred W. Coope, *A Bottom-Up Assessment of Navy Flagship Schools: The NPS Faculty Critique of CNA's Report*, Monterey, Calif.: Naval Postgraduate School, 1998.

Hanser, Lawrence M., Louis W. Miller, Herbert J. Shukiar, and Bruce Newsome, *Developing Senior Navy Leaders: Requirements for Flag Officer Expertise Today and in the Future*, Santa Monica, Calif.: RAND Corporation, MG-618-NAVY, 2008. As of June 4, 2010:
http://www.rand.org/pubs/monographs/MG618/

Hardison, Chaitra M., and Anna-Maria Vilamovska, *The Collegiate Learning Assessment: Setting Standards for Performance at College or University*, Santa Monica, Calif.: RAND Corporation, TR-663-CAE, 2009. As of June 4, 2010:
http://www.rand.org/pubs/technical_reports/TR663/

Harvey, VADM J. C., Jr., Officer Graduate Education Service Obligation, message NAVADMIN 195/07, August 7, 2006.

Hunton, James E., Dan N. Stone, and Benson Wier, "Does Graduate Business Education Contribute to Professional Accounting Success?" *Accounting Horizons,* Vol 19, No. 2, 2005, pp. 85–100.

James, Jeffrey W., *Analysis of Subspecialty Utilization of Naval Officers with a Focus on Time Spent in Subspecialty Tours*, thesis, Monterey, Calif.: Naval Postgraduate School, 1995.

Jordan, Susan S., *An Analysis of the Impact of Graduate Education on the Performance and Retention of General Unrestricted Line Officers*, Monterey, Calif.: Naval Postgraduate School, 1991.

Lawler, Edward E., "From Job-Based to Competency-Based Organizations," *Journal of Organizational Behavior,* Vol. 15, No. 1, 1994, pp. 3–15.

Lianez, Raul, and Luis R. Zamarripa, "The Effects of U.S. Marine Corps Officer Graduate Education Programs on Officer Performance: A Comparative Analysis of Professional Military Education and Graduate Education," thesis, Monterey, Calif.: Naval Postgraduate School, 2003.

Lorio, Jennifer L., "An Analysis of the Effect of Surface Warfare Officer Continuation Pay (SWOCP) on the Retention of Quality Officers," thesis, Monterey, Calif.: Naval Postgraduate School, 2006.

Marine Corps Order 1520.9G, Special Education Program (SEP), Department of the Navy, July 21, 2003.

Marine Corps Order 1560.19E, Advanced Degree Program (ADP), Department of the Navy, June 25, 2003.

MCO—*See* Marine Corps Order.

McPeck, John E., "Critical Thinking and the 'Trivial Pursuit' Theory of Knowledge" in Kerry S. Walters, ed., *Re-Thinking Reason New Perspectives in Critical Thinking,* Albany: State University of New York Press, 1994, pp. 101–117.

Mehay, Stephan L., and William R. Bowman, "Analysis of the Return on Investment (ROI) on Navy Immediate Graduate Education Programs," paper presented at the Annual Navy Workforce Conference, 2007.

Milner, Christopher G., "A Cost-Benefit Analysis of Early Graduate Education Programs for U.S. Naval Academy Graduates," thesis, Monterey, Calif.: Naval Postgraduate School, 2003.

Mithas, Sunial, and M. S. Krishnan, "Human Capital and Institutional Effects in the Compensation of Information Technology Professionals in the United States," *Management Science*, Vol. 54, No. 3, 2008, pp. 415–428.

Moskowitz, M. J., A. D. Parcell, et al., *Developing an Expeditionary Warfare Officer Career Path*, Alexandria, Va.: Center for Naval Analyses, 2009.

Moskowitz, M. J., D. M. Rodney, et al., *Data Analysis for a Navy Education Strategy*, Alexandria, Va.: Center for Naval Analyses, 2008.

Nahapiet, Janine, and Sumantra Ghoshal, "Social Capital, Intellectual Capital, and the Organizational Advantage," *The Academy of Management Review*, Vol. 23, No. 2, April 1998, pp. 242–266.

Naval Postgraduate School, Factbook, Monterey, Calif., 2005.

Navy Personnel Command website, OCEANO detailer's pages, undated. As of December 21, 2009:
http://www.npc.navy.mil/Npc/Templates/FAQSummary

NPS—*See* Naval Postgraduate School.

Office of the Chief of Naval Operations (OPNAV) Instruction 1520.23B, Graduate Education, October 1, 1991.

———, 1500.72F, Navy Politico-Military Fellowships and Graduate Education Programs, June 11, 2007.

———, 1520.42, Advanced Education Governance, May 18, 2009.

Oreopoulos, Philip, and Kjell G. Salvanes, "How Large Are Returns to Schooling? Hint: Money Isn't Everything," working paper, Cambridge, Mass.: National Bureau of Economic Research, September 2009.

Petraeus, David H., "Beyond the Cloister," *The American Interest*, July–August 2007. As of June 30, 2010:
http://www.the-american-interest.com/article.cfm?piece=290

Phillips, Jack J., Ron D. Stone, and Patricia Pulliam Phillips, *The Human Resources Scorecard: Measuring the Return on Investment*, Boston: Butterworth-Heinemann, 2001.

Powell, Seth K., "'Train for the Known, Educate for the Unknown': The Navy's Struggle for Clarity with Graduate Education in the Humanities, from Holloway to Rickover," *International Journal of Naval History*, Vol. 4, No. 2, 2004.

Putnam, Robert D., "Tuning In, Tuning Out: The Strange Disappearance of Social Capital in America," *Political Science and Politicas,* Vol 28, No. 4, 1995.

Roth, John P., FY 2009 Department of Defense (DoD) Military Personnel Composite Standard Pay and Reimbursement Rates, memorandum, Washington, D.C.: Office of the Under Secretary of Defense, 2009. As of July 15, 2010: http://comptroller.defense.gov/rates/fy2009/2009_k.pdf

Schuller, T., S. Baron, and J. Field, "Social Capital: A Review and Critique," in S. Baron, J. Field, and T. Schuller, eds., *Social Capital: Critical Perspectives*, Oxford: Oxford University Press, 2000, pp. 1–38.

Scott, Lynn M., Steve Drezner, Rachel Rue, and Jesse Reyes, *Compensating for Incomplete Domain Knowledge*, Santa Monica, Calif.: RAND Corporation, DB-517-AF, 2007. As of June 4, 2010: http://www.rand.org/pubs/documented_briefings/DB517/

U.S. Government Accountability Office, *Human Capital: A Guide for Assessing Strategic Training and Development Efforts in the Federal Government*, GAO-03-893G, 2003.

U.S. Navy, Bureau of Naval Personnel, *Manual of Navy Officer Manpower and Personnel Classifications*, Vol 1., *Major Code Structures*, NAVPERS 15839I, July 2010. As of June 30, 2010: http://www.npc.navy.mil/NR/rdonlyres/1AC16BAB-3F37-4331-8178-C69566AB7A82/0/NOCVol1.pdf